IF THE PASTA WIGGLES, DON'T EAT IT...
AND OTHER GOOD ADVICE

If the Pasta Wiggles, Don't Eat It... And Other Good Advice

▲▼▲

*Wise Words to Tickle Your Funny Bone
and Make You Think*

Martha Bolton

Servant Publications
Ann Arbor, Michigan

Vine Books is an imprint of Servant Publications especially designed to serve evangelical Christians.

All Scripture references, unless otherwise noted, are taken from the Holy Bible, New International Version. © 1973, 1978, 1984 International Bible Society. Used by permission of Zondervan Bible Publishers.

Published by Servant Publications
P.O. Box 8617
Ann Arbor, Michigan 48107

Cover illustration by Pat Binder
Cover and text design by Diane Bareis

02 03 04   15 14

Printed in the United States of America
ISBN 0-89283-852-3

Library of Congress Cataloging-in-Publication Data

Bolton, Martha, 1951-
   If the pasta wiggles, don't eat it—and other good advice : wise words that tickle your funny bone and make you think / Martha Bolton.
      p.   cm.
   ISBN 0-89283-852-3
   1. Teenager—Prayer–books and devotions—English.   2.
Devotional calendars—Juvenile literature.   [1. Prayer books and devotions.   2. Devotional calendars.]   I. Title.
BV4850.B63   1995
242'.63—dc20
                                              94-41974
                                                 CIP

Dedication

To the three youths who live at my house—
Russ, Matt, and Tony
and
To all the other youths who almost live at my house—
Thanks for the honor of being called "Mom."

Contents

Who Am I?

Follow the Leader

Acknowledgments

▲ ▼ ▲

A special thanks to:
My husband, Russ, who says our marriage still has
plenty of fire—in our oven, our toaster, our broiler,
our microwave...

To my parents, Lonnie and Eunice Ferren, who demon-
strated that the best way to live life is with a sense of
humor, a giving heart, and a strong faith in God.

To my friends at Servant Books, especially Liz Heaney,
whose daily wake up calls kept me on track and
(almost) on schedule.

And finally, to teens everywhere who've either bought
this book, received it as a gift, or rescued it from use
as a doorstop in their church library, I *appreciate* it!

Introduction

▲ ▼ ▲

Life is about relationships. Our relationships with our family, friends, and the not-so-friendly. Our relationship with ourselves. And our relationship with the Lord.

The focus of this three-month devotional is on those relationships. It's designed to be read a chapter a day, but if you've had the absolute worst twenty-four hours of your life it's okay to go ahead and read another chapter, or even three or four more chapters. The Devotional Police aren't going to come to your house and cite you for exceeding the page limit. They can, however, arrest you for failing to heed a laugh line, so be sure not to let that happen.

At the end of each chapter, there are questions to ponder, a daily Scripture, and a prayer. There's also a "Bumper Sticker for the Day," and you don't even have to tailgate anyone to read it.

The most important thing is just to enjoy these next three months that we spend together. When you're through, I hope you'll have laughed some, grown some, and realized that if the pasta wiggles, maybe you really *shouldn't* eat it.

Part One

▲▼▲

Hey, How'd *They* Get on My Prayer List?

This first section deals with our relationships with our loved ones, as well as those people we're desperately *trying* to love. From handling bullies to shunning gossip to giving friends the benefit of the doubt, these readings cover it all... well, almost all. There isn't a chapter on your relationship with your pet. I had one, but my dog chewed it up. I guess he figured it'd go down easier than my leftovers.

One
▲▼▲

Mouth Closed
for Repairs

Have you ever said something that you regretted the minute the words left your lips? Or stayed in a conversation long after your brain walked out? I have. Sometimes I talk a lot more than I listen, which is contrary to God's design. He made our mouths to close, but not our ears. He was probably making a point.

My mouth gets me into much more trouble than my ears do. Like the time I told a policeman, "I didn't run that red light! I ran the two stop signs before it, but I distinctly remember *not* running that red light!"

Or when I explained to my English teacher that the reason my book report on *Jane Erye* was late was because the Cliffs Notes were already checked out of the library and all the video stores were out of the movie version.

I probably would have offered Jonah fishsticks for dinner; and said to George Washington, "Don't lug that jacket around with you. How cold could Valley Forge get?"

If it's the wrong thing to say, I'll usually say it. I am getting better, though. I passed someone yesterday who was the spitting image of Mel Gibson. But I bit my tongue and didn't say a single word. It was better that way. After all, I had no idea how she'd take it.

Thoughts to Ponder:

Write about something you've said, but regretted.

Were you able to take it back? Why or why not?

What did you learn from that experience about the importance of what comes out of our mouths?

Bumper Sticker for the Day:

A mouth isn't a convenience store.
It wasn't meant to stay open
twenty-four hours a day.

Scripture to Stand On:

"He who guards his mouth and his tongue keeps himself
from calamity."   PROVERBS 21:23

Hello again, Lord...

Lord, help me to remember that when You designed my
mouth, You didn't intend my foot to spend so much time in
it.

Two
▲▼▲

Death by
Embarrassment

Do you know that no one dies of embarrassment? It may feel like a terminal condition, but let a little time pass, and usually your embarrassment will go with it.

I've had more than my share of embarrassing situations. Like the time I ran into a well-known television weatherman at a local fast food restaurant. We knew each other professionally, and he invited me to join him for lunch. We laughed, we talked, we had a great time. When his lunch time was over, he went back to the studio and I went back to my car. When I looked in the rear view mirror to back up, I saw that it was clear. My face, however, wasn't. There, adhered to my right cheek, was a large chunk of cheese! I've tried to avoid eye contact with that weatherman ever since. Even when he's on the television screen!

Then there was the time I ran out of gas. I had only been driving a few weeks, and as I stood there emptying a five-gallon can of gasoline into my car, a man stopped to ask what I was doing. I explained my car had run out of gas.

"Then why in the world are you putting gas in the radiator!" he gasped, quickly snatching the gas can from my hand, no doubt saving my engine.

It wasn't my fault. I just assumed that big thing under the hood with the cap on it was the gas tank. Every time my parents pulled into a station for a fill-up, the attendant would open the hood. I figured that's where he was putting the gas. (Back then, gas station attendants would actually open the hood!)

Yes, life is full of embarrassing situations that make us want to crawl in a hole and hide out until the Lord comes. But we can't do that. We've got to go on, face our blunders, and take comfort in the fact that in time everyone will forget. These two stories I've shared are ancient history now. Everyone involved has forgotten all about them. Or had, until I just brought them up again.

Hmmmm... on second thought, maybe I should leave this chapter out.

Thoughts to Ponder:

Write about your most embarrassing moment.
✎

Are you able to laugh about it now? Why do you think the passage of time helps to ease the pain of embarrassment?
✎

Bumper Sticker for the Day:
Sometimes blushing is painful,
but it's saved me a fortune in rouge.

Scripture to Stand On:
"Thou *art* my hiding place and my shield: I hope in thy word."
PSALM 119:114 (KJV)

Hello Again, Lord...
Lord, thank You that, even in my most embarrassing moments,
I can hide in Your love.

Three

▲▼▲

Bad Connections

It was one of those newspaper headlines you never forget: "Local pioneer in good health at the time of his death."

I couldn't help but wonder—if he was in such good health, why was he dead?

I'm sure the reporter didn't mean it the way it sounded. But miscommunications do happen. Someone says or does something that doesn't come across quite the way it was intended.

It's like what sometimes happens at drive-through restaurants. You order a cheeseburger, fries and a Coke, but the server hears a fish sandwich, onion rings, two tacos and a chocolate shake.

Communication is important. It's important to speak clearly and listen carefully. Wars have broken out because of mere misunderstandings. Friendships have been ruined, and over time marriages have failed because someone wasn't listening closely enough or communicating his or her thoughts clearly.

So before you respond, make sure you not only heard what was said, but also what was meant. And when you speak, make sure you're saying what you want to say. After all, unless you're trying to rebuild the Tower of Babel, there's no reason not to communicate.

Thoughts to Ponder:

Have you ever misunderstood something that someone said? Explain.

Has someone ever misunderstood what you were trying to say? Tell about it.

Why do you think it's important to listen to each other?

Bumper Sticker for the Day:

A bad connection can create a lot
of static in your life.

Scripture to Stand On:

"He who answers before listening—that is his folly and his shame." PROVERBS 18:13

Hello Again, Lord...

Lord, help me to communicate *better* with those around me, and *more often* with You.

Four
▲▼▲

A Sorry State of Affairs

The most difficult word to pronounce in the English language isn't "supercalifragilisticexpialidocious." It isn't "antidisestablishmentarianism" either. The most difficult word to pronounce has only five letters, but it's a real tongue twister. It must be. Why else would so many of us have such a hard time saying it?

The word? "S-o-r-r-y."

Now, you would think a word that size would be a cinch to pronounce, but it isn't. Some people won't even attempt to say it. Others practically choke on each syllable. Even some of those who do get it out are so unsure of the pronunciation that they merely whisper it.

"Sorry" isn't always hard to say, though. There are some occasions when it just rolls right off our tongues, distinct as you please. This usually happens when the word is used in one of the following sentences:

"Are *you* ready to say *you're* sorry?"

"*You're* the one who should be sorry."

"*You're* sorry? Well, *you* certainly should be sorry!"

When the word is used in that context, the correct pronunciation comes easily. The accent falls in exactly the right places. There's no stuttering or hesitation whatsoever.

But change the accompanying word *you* to an *I*, and you'd think sorry was a foreign expression. People start mumbling, stammering, coughing.

We really should practice saying "I'm sorry" as much as we can. It's one of the most powerful phrases in the English language. It can heal broken friendships and broken families. It might even be a big step toward world peace.

Given its power, you'd think we'd use it a lot more often than we do.

Thoughts to Ponder:

Why do you think the word sorry is so hard to say sometimes?

Do you know any broken relationships that could be mended by the use of the word sorry? Explain.

Bumper Sticker for the Day:

The way some people restrict their use of the word *sorry,*
you'd think it was on the endangered species list.

Scripture to Stand On:

"Yet now I am happy, not because you were made sorry, but because your sorrow led you to repentance."

2 CORINTHIANS 7:9

Hello Again, Lord...

Lord, help me to realize that getting out the word "sorry" shouldn't require the Heimlich maneuver.

Five

▲▼▲

Can You
Blame Me?

It's easy to blame others for the things that we do.

"It was Phillip who ate those cookies," we say as Oreo crumbs fly out of our mouths.

"That car accident was the other driver's fault," we whine. "All we did was cross over into their lane."

"We would have passed that test if it hadn't been for our teacher. She asked all the wrong questions—questions that were in the book, in her lectures, in her handouts. Questions that would have required some studying on our part. Go figure."

People have been blaming others for their own wrongdoings and shortcomings since the beginning of time. When God cornered Adam in the Garden of Eden to question his disobedience, Adam quickly passed the blame, not just to Eve, but back to God as well.

"It was that woman *You* gave me. It's all *her* fault!"

Eve wasn't about to accept any responsibility either.

"It was the serpent's fault," she said. "I was just walking along, minding my own business, looking for something different to eat, you know, instead of the same ol', same ol' 'bountiful feast' sort of thing, when that ol' snake called out to me and tempted me to taste of the fruit of the forbidden tree. It seemed to fit in with my low-fat, high-fiber diet, so I figured why not?"

Blaming others may be a convenient way to avoid responsibility for our own actions, but in the long run we're only hurting ourselves, denying our need for forgiveness, and stunting our spiritual growth. Accepting our failures and sins and learning from them is how we mature. It's how we can become more like Christ. It's how we train ourselves to make the right decisions next time.

Jesus already paid for our debt of sin when He died on the cross, so is there really any need to keep passing the buck?

Thoughts To Ponder:

Why do you think it's important to accept responsibility for your own actions?

There are many instances in the Bible of people who walked in disobedience with God, then admitted their failure, asked forgiveness, and went on to become great men or women of God. Can you name one or more?

What do you think they learned about accepting responsibility for their own sin?

Bumper Sticker for the Day:

When it comes to blame, it's not better
to give than it is to receive.

Scripture to Stand On:

"He who conceals his sins does not prosper, but whoever confesses and renounces them finds mercy."   PROVERBS 28:13

Hello Again, Lord...

Lord, help me to realize that blame is like a football.
Sometimes not passing it is the best way to go.

Six
▲▼▲

The Whole Truth

Okay, so it was one little lie. What's the big deal? One teensy weensy little white lie. It shouldn't even be classified as a lie. Not a whole one, anyway. It was like low-fat milk: two percent of the truth was still in there.

Maybe I should start at the beginning.

My best friend asked what I was going to do on Friday night. I told her I'd probably sit at home and watch some television. That wasn't a lie. I didn't say at *whose* home I would be, or *whose* television I would be watching.

I really was going to a slumber party at another friend's home. I couldn't say that, though. After all, who wants to hear about a slumber party they weren't invited to? So I just told this little near-truth, this half-reality, this generic fact.

"You're going to be sitting at home, huh?" my best friend questioned, displaying just a hint of suspicion.

"Yes," I reaffirmed. *"Why?"*

"Oh, I was just wondering," she said, then turned and walked away.

Whew! I sighed to myself. I'd gotten away with it. I could now go to the party without her knowing. If I told her the whole truth she might want me to try to get her invited, and to be perfectly honest, this just wasn't her crowd. They were the more popular girls. I wasn't even sure why I was invited, but I didn't want to do anything to jeopardize my good fortune.

As much as possible, I avoided my best friend for the rest of the week. I didn't want to be cornered into confessing the truth.

When Friday finally arrived, I rolled up my sleeping bag, packed my pajamas and my arsenal of practical jokes, dodged two more telephone calls from my best friend, and took off for the party.

As I rang the doorbell, I could hear everyone laughing and carrying on inside. It was going to be a *great* party. I just knew it!

When the door opened, I quickly began to have my doubts.

"I didn't know you were going to be here," my best friend said, giving me an excited hug.

"I didn't know *you* were going to be here," I mumbled nervously.

"I kept hinting all week to see if you were coming," she explained. "I even called you twice today. I didn't want to say anything about the party if you weren't invited, but if you were, I thought we could ride together or something. How come you didn't tell me the truth?"

My mind zipped through a myriad of possible excuses— none of them good enough.

"I'm sorry," I said. "I was wrong. I should have told you I was coming. But we're too good of friends to let this come between us, right?"

"Isn't that the truth!" she smiled, her voice barely carrying over the music.

"It will be from now on," I promised.

Thoughts to Ponder:

Have you ever been caught in a lie? Explain.

How hard was it to undo the damage your lie caused?

How does God feel about lying?

Bumper Sticker for the Day:

When it comes to little white lies or
those of any other shade, God is color-blind.

Scripture to Stand On:

"Therefore each of you must put off falsehood and speak
truthfully to his neighbor, for we are all members of one
body."   EPHESIANS 4:25

Hello Again, Lord...

Lord, help me to remember that lies are like balloons. The
more hot air I add to them, the bigger they get.

Seven

▲▼▲

Warning:
Grouch Ahead

Wouldn't it be great if people came with attitude alarms? As soon as someone got into a bad mood, an alarm would sound, warning us to stay away. We'd never again have to accidentally run into someone who got up on the cranky side of the bed.

Grumpy people can be really hard to take. You tell them to have a nice day, they tell you to mind your own business. You comment on the beautiful springlike weather, they complain about their allergies. You ask them for their advice and they advise you to bug off. Why, some people are so grumpy, they'd have to hang upside down just to turn their frowns into smiles.

I don't know who I'd talk to about inventing an alarm like this, but I believe the idea has merit. Imagine it: with attitude alarms, you'd be able to avoid that snarling salesclerk, that testy teacher, that worn-out waitress. You'd know the best time to show your parents your report card or request that raise in your allowance. You'd be able to gauge the perfect moment to ask to borrow your sister's sweater or your brother's new jeans. Why, an alarm like this could revolutionize relationships!

Until someone invents it, though, we'll just have to go on dealing with people in not-so-pleasant moods. We don't have to let their bad attitudes affect ours, however. We should learn from the zookeepers. Just because they're around growling animals all day long doesn't mean they have to join in the chorus.

Thoughts to Ponder:

Why do you think it's important to maintain a good attitude?

✎

What do you think your attitude says about your relationship with Christ?

✎

Bumper Sticker for the Day:

If God had intended us to go through life
barking at each other, He would have given us
four legs, fur and a tail.

Scripture to Stand On:

"Do not make friends with a hot-tempered man, do not associate with one easily angered, or you may learn his ways and get yourself ensnared."   PROVERBS 22:24-25

Hello Again, Lord...

Lord, help my attitude to depend on no one's but Yours.

Eight
▲ ▼ ▲

An Encouraging
Word

Several times a year, our church youth group plays a game we call "An Encouraging Word." It goes like this: Each youth in attendance writes his or her name on a small piece of paper. We collect all the papers in an offering plate, then pass the plate around the room. As each person draws someone's name from the plate, he or she has to say an encouraging word to that person. The only rule is that all comments *must* be positive.

It's one of our youth group's favorite games. Friends get to share things they've never said before to each other. Sisters and brothers get to hear their siblings say how much they admire and care about them, instead of the usual comments such as, "How long are you going to be in that bathroom?" and "Did you have to set your blow dryer down next to my hamster cage? His hair's now standing on end and I just clocked his carousel at seventy-three miles per hour!"

Positive words are powerful. If you don't believe me, ask some successful people what made them start believing they could achieve their goals in life. More often than not, they'll quote a single comment made by a friend, relative, or even a stranger. A few words gave them the confidence they needed to succeed. That's the power of an encouraging word.

Too often we *think* positive thoughts about each other, but fail to vocalize them. Unspoken encouragement doesn't do anybody any good. So why not impact someone's life forever? Spread a little encouragement. It's free and guaranteed to last a lifetime.

Thoughts to Ponder:

What's the most encouraging thing that someone has said to you? Have you told that person what his or her comment meant to you?

Think of an encouraging word you can share with someone today.

Bumper Sticker of the Day:

Our words are like elevators.
They're either going to lift people up
or bring them down.

Scripture to Stand On:

"Let us encourage one another." HEBREWS 10:25B

Hello Again, Lord...

Lord, all words have power. Help mine to have a positive charge.

Nine
▲▼▲

Who's Afraid of
the Big Bad Bully?

We all have to deal with bullies from time to time. But the worst bully we'll ever face doesn't compare with the one David confronted in 1 Samuel 17. His name was Goliath and he was a giant of a bully. He challenged the entire Israelite army to take him on. Not one soldier volunteered. Evidently boot camp didn't include training in hand-to-hand combat with a tank.

But then David stepped into the scene. This young shepherd boy had already killed a lion and a bear with his bare hands. He figured Goliath wouldn't be any more difficult to bring down. His breath might be worse, but defeating him wouldn't be any harder.

And he was right. David stood up to Goliath and down the giant came. Why? Because David was such a great warrior? No. Because he knew the Lord was with him and he stood his ground.

The Lord is with us when we face the "bullies" in our lives—whether they're people, obsessions, addictive behaviors, or whatever we allow to control us.

The next time a bully pushes you around, just remember—he wouldn't be talking so big if he could see who's standing behind you.

Thoughts to Ponder:

Is there something controlling your life? What is it?

How can God help you get out from under its control?

Bumper Sticker for the Day:

Bullies don't look so big after they've been conquered.

Scripture to Stand On:

"Therefore put on the full armor of God, so that when the day of evil comes, you may be able to stand your ground."

EPHESIANS 6:13A

Hello Again, Lord...

Lord, I have nothing to fear, for You're bigger than any giant I'll ever have to face.

Ten
▲ ▼ ▲

Brick Walls

Have you ever noticed that brick walls don't budge? I learned that the hard way when I accidentally drove into the wall of our church. The wall didn't move, but the side panel of my car did. I tried explaining to my parents that I shouldn't be punished because it was a "holy" accident, but they wouldn't buy it.

The accident did teach me something, though. Something about brick walls. They're stubborn. They don't yield, they don't bend. No matter how much damage they do to others, they're not about to move for anyone.

Some people can be like brick walls—so cemented in their own opinions and viewpoints that when someone dares to confront them, it's a collision. It's their way or no way. They're always right, never wrong. They know it all and will try to control it all.

This type of person has a hard time keeping friends because getting along with others means being flexible sometimes. If you hate baseball, but all your friends are avid fans and want to go to the game on Friday night, you can't just dig in your heels and insist everybody go roller skating instead. If you do, you could end up being the only one on the skating floor.

Don't get me wrong. On some things we *should* stand firm. We shouldn't compromise our morals and standards. But insisting on watching the movie *we* want to watch, or doing the activity *we* want to do, or just having things *our* way isn't the proper attitude. We need to take other people's feelings and desires into consideration. After all, even brick walls seem a lot more friendly when there's a gate.

Thoughts to Ponder:

When you're around people who insist on doing things *their* way, how does it make you feel?

Why do you think it's important to consider other people's feelings when making decisions?

Bumper Sticker for the Day:
People who always dig in their heels
end up with a lot of blisters.

Scripture to Stand On:
"Do nothing out of selfish ambition or vain conceit, but in humility consider others better than yourselves."   PHILIPPIANS 2:3

Hello Again, Lord...
Lord, when it comes to my relationships with others, help me not to build brick walls.

Eleven
▲▼▲

The Name Game

I inherited a few nicknames in school. The first one was "Olive Oyl." I tried seeing it in a positive light— Olive Oyl was a star, she had two men fighting over her, and her hair was always in place. That's not why I got the nickname, though. It was because I was tall, lanky, and had feet so big I needed *two* surfboards to surf.

Years later, my nickname changed, but not for the better. After using a vibrator belt on my arms in an attempt to tone my muscles, I awoke the next morning to find that the muscles were indeed toned. All of my upper arm fat had slid down to my elbows, but my muscles were toned. Don't ask me how or why my fat decided to head south, but it happened. It was an unexplainable medical oddity. I ended up with bone-thin upper arms and ballooning forearms. My new nickname? You guessed it— "Popeye."

I tried not to let that name get to me either. I simply made the best of a weird situation. After all, "I yam what I yam."

It took two years for my arms to return to normal, and equally as long for my new nickname to go away. (Of course, my wearing bellbottoms and talking with one eye closed didn't help matters.)

Still, my nicknames never really bothered me. I knew being called Popeye or Olive Oyl wasn't going to turn me into the cartoon superstars. No one would stop me on the street and ask for my autograph. The studios wouldn't mail me any residual checks for my reruns. That's because nicknames can't change who we are inside. You can call a rosebush a tumble-weed all day long, but that's not going to make it a tumble-weed. (Although, in my garden, it's hard to tell them apart!)

Thoughts to Ponder:

Do you know someone who's been given a negative nick-name? How could that nickname be damaging?

How can you help turn that situation into something more positive?

Bumper Sticker of the Day:

A rose by any other name would be a lot harder to spell.

Scripture to Stand On:

"You will be called by a new name that the mouth of the Lord will bestow."   Isaiah 62:2b

Hello Again, Lord...

Lord, thank You for looking beyond our labels and seeing who's really inside.

Twelve

▲▼▲

Sibling Quibbling

Have you ever had a disagreement with your brother or sister?

"She borrowed my jeans without asking!"

"He's always picking on me!"

"Make her hang up. She's been on that phone since August!"

Whatever conflict you may experience, it pales in comparison to what Joseph endured from his brothers (see Genesis 37-45). Joseph's brothers were so jealous of him that they threw him into a pit, then sold him into slavery. Nice guys, huh? I don't know about you, but it would sure ruin my day if my brother did that. It would also be pretty hard to forgive him.

Yet even though Joseph's brothers did him wrong, God made good come from their actions. Through a series of remarkable events, Joseph gained his freedom and was eventually promoted to work as Pharaoh's second-in-command over all of Egypt.

When famine hit the area and Joseph's brothers were in a position of need, they came to Joseph for help. What a perfect time for Joseph to take his revenge. What a perfect time to have them thrown into a pit or sold as slaves like he was. But he didn't do any of that. He didn't run his version of the story in the *Egyptian Enquirer* or appear on the "Sally Cleopatra Raphael Show" on sibling rivalry. What did he do? He forgave them.

If Joseph could forgive his brothers for all they did to him, overlooking a borrowed pair of jeans or waiting a little longer for Sis to clear that phone line doesn't seem so hard, does it?

Thoughts to Ponder:

Why do you think Joseph was able to forgive his brothers for all the wrongs they had done to him?

✎

The Bible tells us we're to forgive seventy times seven (Mt 18:21-22). Just how many times is that?

✎

Bumper Sticker for the Day:

Sometimes evening up the score
just means you go from winning to a tie.

Scripture to Stand On:

"Be kind and compassionate to one another, forgiving each other, just as in Christ God forgave you."   EPHESIANS 4:32

Hello Again, Lord...

Lord, help me to forgive with the same heart that You forgive me.

Thirteen
▲▼▲

What's Trust Got
to Do with It

I searched my purse again. The money wasn't in my wallet, it wasn't in the zippered compartment, it wasn't tucked away in my makeup pouch.

The evidence was clear. This morning I put a twenty dollar bill in my wallet and now it was gone. The only person who had been near my purse was my best friend. But why would *she* take my money? It didn't make any sense. I had no choice but to get out of the cafeteria line and go on a mandatory fast.

"Here, let me buy today," my friend said, as I started to walk away.

"Thanks," I forced a smile. "I really appreciate it." What I really wanted to say was, "I'd appreciate it if you'd give me my twenty bucks!"

She bought me a cheeseburger, fries and a Coke. Pretty generous, but then again, it *was* my money.

All through lunch I listened as she told me how much our friendship had helped her. (Of course it's helped her, I thought to myself. It's made her twenty bucks richer!) She went on and on about the merits of a true friend and how important it is not to do anything to jeopardize that relationship. Finally I couldn't stand it any longer.

"Well," I began, my neck muscles tensing. "Since you brought it up, I'd like to add that a *true* friend is someone who would never..."

Taking a dramatic pause, I slid my right hand into my pants pocket and leaned back on one foot for even further effect. She *knew* where I was going with this. She *knew* I was going to say that a true friend is someone who would never take twenty dollars from you, someone you can trust.

Just as I was about to utter those words, I felt something in my pocket. As I pulled it out, I could see it was green, it was paper, it was my twenty dollar bill.

"You were saying...?" my friend pressed.

I could feel my cheeks flushing as I swallowed hard and thanked God I hadn't finished.

"I was saying a true friend is someone who would never believe anything but the best about you.... Come on, I'll buy dessert."

That day I learned something about jumping to conclusions. There's always a risk of landing on the wrong side of the truth.

Thoughts to Ponder:

Have you ever been suspected of something you didn't do? How did it make you feel?

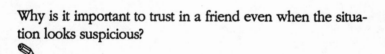

Why is it important to trust in a friend even when the situation looks suspicious?

Bumper Sticker for the Day:

Sometimes the best gift you can give a friend
is the benefit of the doubt.

Scripture to Stand On:

"A friend loves at all times."   PROVERBS 17:17A

Hello Again, Lord...

Lord, help me to be the last to see a fault in a friend, and not
the first.

Fourteen
▲ ▼ ▲

Just Joking

"**A**re those your ears or hang-gliding equipment?"

"Love your hair. Who styled it? Hurricane Andrew?"

"Where'd you get those shoes? Bozo have a garage sale?"

"You call those muscles? I've had blisters bigger than that."

The problem with teasing someone is knowing when to stop. Oh, maybe the first line gets a laugh, perhaps even a comeback, but sooner or later, feelings get hurt.

The Bible warns us against coarse, hurtful joking. Ephesians 5:4 lists some of the things that are improper for God's holy people to do: "Nor should there be obscenity, foolish talk or coarse joking, which are out of place." God doesn't want us to say hurtful things to each other. This doesn't mean we can't laugh and have a good time. God created us with the ability to laugh. He wants us to be joyful, but our laughter shouldn't be at the expense of someone else.

Remember the root of *funny* is fun. Our humor should lighten the moment. It should leave people feeling good. Above all, it should be *fun*... for everyone, not just the person telling the joke.

Thoughts to Ponder:

Have you ever been hurt by someone's joking? How did you feel?

Have you ever hurt someone by going too far with your teasing? How do you think it made that person feel?

Bumper Sticker for the Day:

A good joke should ease tension,
not create it.

Scripture to Stand On:

"If any man offend not in word, the same *is* a perfect man, *and* able also to bridle the whole body."   James 3:2B (KJV)

Hello Again, Lord...

Lord, fill my mouth with laughter and my heart with sensitivity.

Fifteen
▲▼▲

God's Love Connection

Waiting for that special someone to show up? Think you already found your perfect match? Here's a secret for finding and keeping a good relationship—concentrate on your relationship with someone else. Not just *anyone* else. Concentrate on your relationship with the Lord.

Any relationship that has God at its center has what it takes to last. You'll still have rocky times, of course. You'll have good times, too. But when you honor God by placing Him first in your life, the good times will be that much better, and you'll have a special strength for those not-so-good times.

If there's no one special in your life right now, don't worry. God knows who is supposed to share your future with you. Be patient. That someone will be along before you know it. Or perhaps it's going to be just you and God for a while, so you can get to know Him better. Who knows what He has planned for your life?

Put your relationship with God first. The other relationships will happen in His time. God created romance. He understands it. You can trust Him with your heart.

Thoughts to Ponder:

Why do you think God cares about our relationships?

✎

When we place our relationship with God first, how can we know that He will take care of everything else?

✎

Bumper Sticker for the Day:

Prince (and Princess) Charming don't come
from toads, but from God.

Scripture to Stand On:

"But seek first his kingdom and his righteousness, and all these things will be given to you as well."   MATTHEW 6:33

Hello Again, Lord...

Lord, help me to trust You with matters of my heart.

Sixteen
▲▼▲

Cutting
Some Slack

By now you've probably noticed parents aren't perfect. We make mistakes. We can be overly strict when the situation calls for leniency. We can be too lenient when we should be strict. We're learning.

Most parents do what they do only because they want what's best for their children. Chore assignments may seem like the ultimate drag to a teen, but to a parent they're a great way to teach self-discipline. (They also keep the nation's ants from holding their annual convention under your bed.)

Your curfew may not make any sense to you, but to a parent who paces the floor worrying, it makes perfect sense. My mother couldn't sleep until she knew I was safe at home (and that continued even after I'd been married twenty years!).

Making you do your homework, wanting to know who your friends are, scheduling a family night, or limiting your telephone time are all for your benefit...whether it seems like it or not. You have to do your homework, unless you want to be gray haired and pushing a walker to your senior prom. Your parents have to limit your telephone time. After all, they don't want you appearing in your class pictures with a receiver to your ear. If you ask them, you might be surprised to find out they have good reasons for their rules.

Remember, it's not parents versus teenagers. We're all on the same team. We might fumble the ball from time to time, you might miss a few passes, but we're all trying to do the best job we can. And we'll eventually make it across the goal line if we work together, pray for each other, and stop for plenty of huddles along the way.

Thoughts to Ponder:

Do your parents have a rule you disagree with? What is it?

You know the reasons why you don't like it. Why do you think your parents feel this rule is important?

What rules have your parents made you obey that you would want your children to obey, too?

Bumper Sticker for the Day:

Surprise your parents—point out something
they're doing right.

Scripture to Stand On:

"Train a child in the way he should go, and when he is old he
will not turn from it."   PROVERBS 22:6

Hello Again, Lord...

Lord, when my parents ask me to take out the trash, help me
to obey... and not give them any garbage.

Seventeen
▲▼▲

Fault Lines

Did you know criticism isn't a ministry? The way a lot of people act, you'd think it's their calling. They can find more faults than a California geologist.

I try not to spend much time around critical people. They wear me down. I can do a hundred things right and they won't say a word. But if I mess up one time, they'll be on my doorstep faster than firemen en route to my kitchen.

Some people try to disguise their negative comments by calling them "constructive criticism."

"You really should wear more makeup. Haven't you heard the 'alive' look is in?"

"Your oral report was great. It helped me catch up on all the sleep I've been missing."

"Your solo was wonderful. You hit all the right notes. Next time, try to hit them in order."

Maybe there is such a thing as constructive criticism, but too often "constructive" criticism is destructive. It's not tempered with sensitivity and it comes from a less-than-helpful heart.

I've worked with many teenagers and I know they can hear compliments all day long, but that one critical comment is what will stick with them. Adults aren't much different.

Sure, we all need to know when we're making a mistake, not putting forth our best effort, or completely lousing up. But wouldn't it be better if we spent our time offering constructive encouragement instead?

Thoughts to Ponder:

How do you think your friends would characterize you—as a criticizer or an encourager?

Why do you think it's important to encourage each other?

Bumper Sticker for the Day:

It's critical to not be critical.

Scripture to Stand On:

"But encourage one another daily."   HEBREWS 3:13A

Hello Again, Lord...

Lord, when you examine my heart, may the prognosis not be "in critical condition."

Eighteen
▲▼▲

Just
Between Friends

It's not easy when you're caught between two friends. This one's not going to your party if that one's going, that one's not going if this one's going, and all you want is for both of them to be there and get along.

It's not really fair when friends sandwich you in the middle of their conflicts. You end up refereeing fights, scheduling peace talks, doing everything you can to make them get along, and still it seems hopeless.

Did you know Jesus had to handle a similar problem? The Bible tells us that on at least one occasion, the disciples disputed among themselves about which one of them would be the greatest in the kingdom of God. It probably didn't go quite like this, but then again, it might as well have:

"Jesus likes me best."

"Does not."

"Does too."

"Does not."

"Does too."

"All right, we're going to settle this once and for all. We'll go ask Him."

"Fine!"

"Jesus, of all Your disciples, which one of us is going to be the greatest in Your kingdom?"

Talk about being put on the spot. Imagine if twelve of your friends approached you with that question.

Jesus had a great answer, though. He said, "He who is least among you all—he is the greatest" (Lk 9:48b).

The arguing stopped right then and there.

Often, when friends compete for our attention, they do it out of jealousy, or insecurity. But Jesus proved that when you make the person in last place the winner, the competition usually ends.

Thoughts to Ponder:

Have your friends ever placed you in the middle of one of their quarrels? Do you think that was fair of them or unfair? Why?

✎

How do you think Jesus felt when his disciples wanted to know which one of them was the greatest?

✎

Bumper Sticker for the Day:
Competition doesn't begin until
someone starts choosing sides.

Scripture to Stand On:
"Finally, all of you, live in harmony with one another; be sympathetic, love as brothers, be compassionate and humble."

1 PETER 3:8

Hello Again, Lord...
Lord, help me to live in unity and to be a friend to all.

Nineteen
▲▼▲

Toxic Tales

Imagine waking up in the middle of the night to the sound of a dump truck making a delivery in your backyard. Quickly grabbing your flashlight, you go outside to investigate, but when you ask the driver what he's dumping, he just smiles and says "toxic waste." Sensing your bewilderment, he goes on to explain that someone left it in his yard, so now he's passing it along to some of his friends and neighbors.

You'd probably tell him to scoop it back up immediately and take it as far away from your house as possible or you're calling the authorities. You'd tell him to never pull a stunt like that again, and wonder why in the world he wanted to share it with you in the first place.

Gossip is like toxic waste. People pass it along secretly, when no one's looking. They don't care how much damage it does. They just want to see how many people they can share it with.

The next time someone tries to dump some toxic gossip in your backyard, tell them to take it right back where it came from. After all, do you really want something that destructive ruining your view?

Thoughts to Ponder:
Why do you think gossip is wrong?

What's a good way to stop someone from passing their gossip along to you?

Bumper Sticker for the Day:
Gossip is *always* 100 percent returnable.

Scripture to Stand On:
"Without wood a fire goes out; without gossip a quarrel dies down."   PROVERBS 26:20

Hello Again, Lord...
Lord, help me to always mark gossip "Return to Sender."

Twenty
▲▼▲

The Cold,
Hard Facts

It was my first time on ice skates.
You could tell by the way I was
skating on the inside of my ankles and using the snack bar
wall to stop.

But I *had* to master this sport. You see, I told my friend
Laura that I could ice skate. Well, actually, I told her I was a
terrific ice skater. She was terrific at everything else. I had to
beat her at something. Since she, too, had never ice skated
before, I figured this was my opportunity.

But I had to hurry. She was going to be at the rink within
the hour. That meant I had to learn to skate and put together
an Olympic-quality routine with spins, jumps and backwards
skating in less than sixty minutes. Could it be done? Nooooo
problem.

Or so I thought.

My first spin spun me into the railing, my jump landed me
on top of the lockers, and the only backwards skating I did
was when I couldn't get out of the way of a speed skater fast
enough and he pushed me around the rink for a couple of
laps.

By the time my friend arrived, the only skill I had mastered
was calling for help.

I had no choice but to swallow my pride and confess that
I'd exaggerated. I'd overstated my talent. I'd stretched the truth
(and a few hamstrings).

Lucky for me, my friend was gracious. She didn't rub my nose in it or anything. I probably wouldn't have felt it even if she had, though. After seven falls, frostbite had set in.

Thoughts to Ponder:

Have you ever bragged about something you couldn't live up to? Explain.

What did you learn from that experience?

Bumper Sticker for the Day:

It's better to tell the truth than to have the truth tell
on you. And that's no exaggeration.

Scripture to Stand On:

"Truthful lips endure forever, but a lying tongue lasts only a moment."

PROVERBS 12:19

Hello Again, Lord...

Lord, help me to remember that stretching the truth can leave me walking on thin ice.

Twenty-One

▲▼▲

Rise and Whine

Do you wake up in a good mood?

I had a friend in high school who used to take a swing at anyone who dared to rouse her before noon. It's no wonder everyone stayed away from her at slumber parties. She *claimed* she was doing all that thrashing about in her sleep and couldn't help it, but that didn't make our bruises heal any faster.

The way I see it, only bears have an excuse for growling in the morning. Why start off the day mad at the world? We've got plenty of time to get cranky, so why rush into it? (Actually, we should try to maintain a good attitude all day long, but if we fail at that endeavor, the least we can do is start our morning right!)

Each new day is a new opportunity—to do better, try a little harder, reach a little further toward our goals. If we made mistakes yesterday, we can try not to make them again today. If nothing's gone right for us all week, perhaps this day will be our turning point. It's a new day, another chance, a brand new beginning.

Now, when we consider how many good things today might have in store, why shouldn't we greet it with a smile?

Thoughts to Ponder:

Describe the kind of mood you usually wake up in.

✐

Do you think waking up in a good mood can have a positive effect on how you handle the rest of your day? Why?

✐

Bumper Sticker for the Day:

There's at least *one* thing to be thankful for
every morning... opening your eyes.

Scripture to Stand On:

"This is the day the Lord has made; let us rejoice and be glad in it."   PSALM 118:24

Hello Again, Lord...

Lord, help me to remember—no one enjoys hearing a bunch of grumbling and complaining first thing in the morning, especially You.

Twenty-two

▲▼▲

Future Wisdom

Did you know that some advice is offered on the layaway plan? You may have no need of it today, but it can be stored in your mind and reserved for some later date. (I use advice today that I laid away years ago—advice that made little sense to me as a teenager but has wisdom I can fully appreciate today.

Someone gave me advice on how to keep a job *before* I even filled out my first resumé, advice on how to handle bills before I ever had any, and advice about marriage long before I ever started dating. (My parents told me the best way to keep my marriage healthy was to "board up the kitchen and eat out.")

I couldn't use much of that advice in the fourth grade, but I still listened. And when the day came that I got a job, got my first bill, and said, "I do," I had a storehouse of good advice to draw from.

When someone gives you good advice, don't tune it out because you don't feel you need it right now. Put it on layaway. Keep it in reserve. Who knows? It could come in very handy someday.

Thoughts to Ponder:

Has someone given you good advice that you plan to use later? What is it?

✎

Why do you think it's wise to have some good advice stored up *before* you need it?

✎

Bumper Sticker for the Day:

The shelf life of good advice is forever.

Scripture to Stand On:

"Hold on to instruction, do not let it go; guard it well, for it is your life."   Proverbs 4:13

Hello Again, Lord...

Lord, help me to accept all the good advice I can—some for today, the rest for tomorrow.

Twenty-three
▲▼▲

Best Friends

In elementary school my best friend and I did everything together. We even ate together (she'd take the good stuff out of my lunch pail, and leave the liverwurst and crackers for me).

By junior high I had a new best friend (I was pretty sick of liverwurst by then). We were close, too. I'd do my homework, she'd take it out of my locker and copy it. I'd buy a new blouse, she'd borrow it. I'd spend the night at her house, she'd make me help clean her room. She wanted to be my best friend for life. I think I know why.

My best friend in high school was another girl. We had a lot in common. We both tried out for the swim team. She made it, I got to clean the pool. We'd go shopping together. She'd shop, I'd carry the packages. After high school, I hardly ever called her anymore. I was too tired to lift the receiver.

Our friends change throughout our lives. They move away. They take up new interests that lead them in a different direction than we're headed. We may even find out they weren't as good of friends as we once thought. The fact is that the person closest to us today may not be closest to us tomorrow.

I have another friend, though, who has never changed and never will. Jesus is always there for me. He's not moody and He's never too busy. He won't use me or take our friendship for granted.

Have you ever felt you could use a friend like that? Someone who loves you even when you're not very lovable? Someone who will never use you or turn His back on you? Someone who thinks so much of you that He even gave His life to prove it? That's a pretty good friend, wouldn't you say? And He's only a prayer away.

Thoughts to Ponder:

What qualities do you look for in a friend?

Have you made Jesus your best friend? What difference has He made in your life?

Bumper Sticker for the Day:

God's love may be free for us, but it cost Him His Son.

Scripture to Stand On:

"Greater love has no one than this, that one lay down his life for his friends." JOHN 15:13

Hello Again, Lord...

Lord, thank You for being a friend I can always count on.

Twenty-four
▲ ▼ ▲

How Does
It Feel?

Have you ever had your feelings hurt by something someone said? You tried to act cool and let the comment roll off your back. You tried not to give the offender the satisfaction of seeing how badly you were hurt. But it was hard—especially when your voice started to crack, your eyes began tearing up, and that awful pain in your chest set in. You know the pain I'm talking about. The one that feels as though your heart is being ripped out of your chest without the benefit of anesthesia. It usually comes whenever you try to fight back tears (or when you down one too many chili cheese dogs).

Hurt feelings can take a long time to heal. An eye can mend itself within days, a broken leg within weeks, but hurt feelings can last a lifetime… if we let them.

When our feelings get hurt, we can do several things. We can retaliate by striking the offender with an even nastier comment. Or we can go to that person and confess that our feelings are hurt. Most people aren't even aware when they've said something hurtful and will readily apologize.

We can replay the incident over and over in our heads, or we can choose not to dwell on it. My mother used to say, "Just push it out of your mind." In other words, don't think about it. Think about other things, like positive comments that people have made.

But the best thing we can do when our feelings get hurt is give them to the Lord. If anyone understands hurt feelings, it's

Jesus. His whole community turned against Him. When He was on trial, not one of His friends came to His defense. Peter even denied knowing him *three* times (Mt 26:69-75).

How did Jesus handle it? Did He snap back? Did He hang on the cross complaining about his situation and the crowd's insensitivity? Did he confront Peter with, "How could you do that to me? And after all I've done for you!" He didn't do any of that. He simply forgave them.

We can't always keep our feelings from getting hurt. But we can control how long we carry the pain.

Thoughts to Ponder:

Tell about a time when your feelings were hurt.

How did you react to it?

Bumper Sticker for the Day:

Insults are like matches—
they'll burn you if you hold them too long.

Scripture to Stand On:

"A man's wisdom gives him patience; it is to his glory to overlook an offense."   PROVERBS 19:11

Hello Again, Lord...

Lord, remind me that what I have to forgive can't even compare to all You had to.

Twenty-five
▲▼▲

Secret Keeper

Did you know it's a compliment when people confide in you? It says they're impressed with your integrity, your discretion, your trustworthiness. It says they know you'll take their problems to the Lord and not to the church bulletin board. You'll keep it in your heart, not cover it on the nightly news.

Even the Bible compliments the person who can be trusted with a secret. It says, "A gossip betrays a confidence, but a trustworthy man keeps a secret" (Prv 11:13).

Unfortunately, for some people keeping a confidence is next to impossible. In fact, the only thing they want to keep secret about a private matter is the identity of the person who's spreading it. "I'll tell you something if you promise not to tell anyone I told you," they'll begin. "I gave my word I wouldn't tell a single soul, so I want your word you'll be very careful whom you tell. If this gets back to my friend she'll never trust me again."

Ummm... I wonder why?

"Can you keep a secret?" doesn't translate to "I'd spread this around to everyone myself, but it'd take too long. Would you be a dear and help me?"

Of course, there are some secrets that shouldn't be kept. If they involve someone's health or safety, then we should seek advice from a pastor, parent, school counselor or other responsible adult. But they're *all* we need to tell. We don't have to share the problem with everyone else on the face of the planet.

The bottom line is that we should live up to the confidence our friends place in us. If they think we're responsible enough to be trusted with their secrets, we shouldn't go out of our way to prove them wrong.

Thoughts to Ponder:

Can your friends confide in you? Why or why not?

Have you ever confided in someone who didn't keep your confidence? How did it make you feel?

Bumper Sticker for the Day:

Some people treat a secret like a cold.
They can't open their mouths without passing it along.

Scripture to Stand On:

"He who covers an offense promotes love, but whoever repeats the matter separates close friends."   PROVERBS 17:9

Hello Again, Lord...

Lord, help me to remember that a confidence isn't like butter. It shouldn't be spread.

Twenty-six
▲▼▲

Pressure Cooker

Have you ever had someone pressure you into doing something you didn't want to do?

"Come on, it'll be fun. Just tell your parents you're spending the night at my house, and I'll tell my parents I'm spending the night at your house. Then we can go to that party and stay as late as we want."

"Let's skip school today after second period. No one will ever know. Trust me."

"Go on, try some. Don't be such a chicken. How bad can Martha's cooking be?"

Even when we know it's the wrong thing to do, even when it puts our own safety and reputation at risk, it's hard to say no when the pressure's on. We want to be liked. We want to be accepted. We're vulnerable.

Satan tried to pressure Jesus into sinning, and he did it at a very vulnerable moment in our Lord's life, too (see Luke 4:1-13). Jesus had just completed a forty-day fast. He was hungry. So guess who happened to show up with a plan for "doing lunch"? Satan said, "If you are the Son of God, tell these stones to become bread."

Notice how he tried to make Jesus think He had something to prove. Often, when the pressure's put on us, it's to get us to prove something, too—that we're not chicken, that we're not nerds, that our friendship is real, or that we're part of the "cool" group.

Jesus knew He had nothing to prove. He was the Son of God whether Satan was prepared to accept that or not. The only person who *did* have something to prove was the one applying the pressure.

We don't have to prove anything to anyone, either. We should already know who we are in Christ. So the next time someone tries to get you to do something wrong to prove your courage, tell them that by saying "no," you just proved it.

Thoughts to Ponder:

Has someone ever tried to pressure you into doing something you know you shouldn't do? How did you handle it?

Why do you suppose some people try to pressure others into doing things they clearly don't want to do?

Bumper Sticker for the Day:

If you *have* to prove something to someone,
prove your loyalty to the Lord.

Scripture to Stand On:

"He who leads the upright along an evil path will fall into his own trap." PROVERBS 28:10A

Hello Again, Lord...

Lord, thank You that I can depend on Your strength... even when the pressure's on.

Twenty-seven

▲▼▲

Go Easy
on Yourself

Ever watch those courtroom scenes on television? The defendant tries to look calm, cool, and collected (which isn't easy to do when you're taking a bath in your own sweat). He knows he's guilty. He knows he's in the hot seat, and his very life may be at stake. So if someone were to come along and offer him a fool-proof plan to make the judge go easy on him, do you think he'd refuse to listen? Of course not. He'd do whatever it took to help lighten his sentence.

According to the Bible, we're the ones who will determine how harshly or how leniently we will be judged. It says "Do not judge, and you will not be judged. Do not condemn, and you will not be condemned. Forgive, and you will be forgiven" (Lk 6:37).

Uh-oh. Maybe we'd better back up and go a little easier on that boy in youth group who stumbled in his Christian walk. Perhaps we should take back everything we said about that girl at school who's been making so many wrong decisions lately. After all, those scathing adjectives we've been using to describe their actions could be used to describe ours someday.

When the woman caught in adultery was brought before Christ, he didn't start condemning her in front of all the people gathered there, citing her life as an example of how wicked some people can become. He said, "Go, and sin no more" (Jn

8:11b, KJV). That's it. No closing arguments summarizing the case against her. No dwelling on her sins and how horrible they were. Christ had nothing but forgiveness.

The next time we can't wait for God to "throw the book" at someone, we need to remember that it's the same book that's going to be judging our lives, too.

Thoughts to Ponder:

What are some reasons why God makes a better judge than we do?

✎

Why do you think it's more important for us to forgive rather than judge?

✎

Bumper Sticker for the Day:

If God had needed our help in judging others,
He would have asked for it.

Scripture to Stand On:

"Therefore let us stop passing judgment on one another."

ROMANS 14:13

Hello Again, Lord...

Lord, help me to leave the judging to You, for You're the only One who knows the heart.

Twenty-eight

▲▼▲

Lockjaw

Do you know people who seem to enjoy getting you into trouble? It's as if they get satisfaction from watching you get punished. They act as though their calling in life is to get you called on the carpet, and they won't rest until they've succeeded and you've failed.

If this sounds familiar, you're not alone. The Bible tells us that Daniel had some jealous people to contend with (see Daniel 6). They hated that fact that King Darius regarded Daniel more highly than them. So they squealed on Daniel. His crime? Praying!

They convinced the king to throw Daniel into the lion's den. Now, I don't know what sort of unjust punishment you've had to face, but it couldn't have been as bad as someone trying to make Lion Chow out of you. Daniel wasn't allowed a jury trial, he wasn't allowed a call to his attorney, he didn't even get a jail cell interview with Donahue.

God was with Daniel, though, and He shut the mouths of those lions so that no harm came to him. It was such a testimony of the power of Daniel's God that the king had Daniel's accusers thrown into the lion's den. This time, however, the lions' mouths were fully operational.

The story had a happy ending for Daniel. Still, it hurts when we realize there are people who don't want the best for us. It hurts, but like Daniel, we don't have to lose any sleep over it.

Not only will God go with us when we face those lions—He will be able to close their mouths, too.

Thoughts to Ponder:

Why might some people not want what's best for us?

✎

Will we ever have to face a situation where God isn't with us? What assurance do we have of this?

✎

Bumper Sticker for the Day:

Only God can turn a lion's den into a petting zoo.

Scripture to Stand On:

"A righteous man may have many troubles, but the Lord delivers him from them all."   PSALM 34:19

Hello Again, Lord...

Lord, thank You that even when the lions are growling, You can block their bite.

Twenty-nine
▲▼▲

Congratulations...
I Think

Have you ever been jealous of someone? Jealous of what they could do that you weren't allowed to do? Jealous of the things they could get that you couldn't?

You've been dreaming of playing on your high school football team for as long as you can remember. But when your friend decides to try out, too, just for the fun of it, he ends up making the team and you don't. You know you should congratulate him, but the words stick in your mouth like refrigerated peanut butter.

It seems every guy on campus likes your friend Cindy, so why does she have to flirt with the *one* guy who's been paying attention to you lately? Can't she just leave him alone and give you a chance to get to know him?

All you've been thinking about is the new surfboard you're going to buy. With every dollar you save, you imagine yourself riding the waves on that beautifully crafted board. But just when you have enough money to buy it, your friend's parents get to the store ahead of you and buy it for your friend for no special occasion whatsoever. You try to act happy for him, but it's hard to smile when your teeth are clinched so tight that your gums almost meet.

It's hard to stand by and watch others get those things we want for ourselves. We can easily think of a hundred reasons why they don't deserve them, and two hundred reasons why *we* do. It only makes matters worse when they seem so unappreciative of their good fortune.

The Bible tells us we're not to worry about things like that. We're to seek God's ways first, and He'll see to it that we receive each and every blessing that is meant for us. True, they may not be the same blessings we've visualized for ourselves. They might be different, and in the long run, better for us.

So don't worry when it seems like other people are getting more of God's blessings than you are. Put God first in your life, and nothing will stop those blessings with your name on them from reaching their final destination.

Thoughts to Ponder:

Have you ever been jealous of something someone else had? What was it?

Do you think God is pleased when we're jealous of others? Why or why not?

Bumper Sticker for the Day:
When it comes from envy,
green is no one's best color.

Scripture To Stand On:
"But seek first his kingdom and his righteousness, and all these things will be given to you as well." MATTHEW 6:33

Hello Again, Lord...
Lord, help me not to dwell on what others have, but on what I have in You.

Thirty
▲▼▲

Hey, How'd *He Get* on My Prayer List?

Is there someone in your life with whom you seem to be in constant conflict? Someone ready to argue with you over everything you say, do, and stand for? Whenever you get together, you're like sticks being rubbed against each other—sooner or later, the sparks start flying. If you say the sun's shining, "Sparky" says it isn't. If you say it's cold, he says it's hot. If you say the traffic light is red, he says it's green... and will *still* be disagreeing with you while the officer is writing out the ticket. How do you handle someone who's gotten on every single nerve in your body, and then some?

You pray for this person.

"You *what?*"

You pray for this person.

"C'mon, get serious."

I am.

"Oh, I get it. Pray he gets laryngitis so he can't say nasty things to me anymore. Or that he moves to another state so he'll stay out of my face."

No. You pray for this person the *same* way you would pray for a friend.

"And just *whose* wise idea was this?" you ask.

The Lord's. Jesus said, "Love your enemies and pray for those who persecute you" (Mt 5:44). But He didn't just *preach*

82

it. He actually *did* it when He hung on that cross and cried, "Father, forgive them, for they do not know what they are doing" (Lk 23:34a).

It's not easy to love people who are constantly on our case. But if we do what the Bible teaches and pray for our enemies as we would our friends, who knows—maybe someday that's just what they will become.

Thoughts to Ponder:

Why do you think it's so hard for us to pray for our enemies?

Why do you think Jesus instructed us to do it, then set the ultimate example of this type of love?

Bumper Sticker for the Day:

"Honk if you're praying for the driver who just cut you off!"

Scripture to Stand On:

"But I tell you who hear me: Love your enemies, do good to those who hate you, bless those who curse you, pray for those who mistreat you."
LUKE 6:27-28

Hello Again, Lord...

Lord, help me to have Your kind of love—the kind that loves those who don't love me back.

Part Two
▲▼▲

Who Am I?

This section deals with our relationship with our-selves—from handling loneliness to overcoming self-doubt to living in joy.

It's important to know who we are, why we do what we do, what we stand for, and what we *won't* stand for. It's good to assess how we're treating others, but it's also good to assess how we're treating ourselves. Are we taking that same advice we give out so freely and applying it to our own life? Are we cutting our-selves as much slack as we're giving others? Are we taking ourselves a little less seriously, and our walk with the Lord a little *more* seriously?

·Who are we? We're about to find out....

Thirty-one
▲▼▲

Laughter
After All

I heard about a man whose tombstone read simply, "Been here. Had a good time. Gone." That inscription says a lot.

We should have a good time in life. The Bible makes many references to how joy and laughter should be part of the Christian walk. I believe that's because our Lord has a pretty good sense of humor Himself.

Remember the story of Baalam and Balak (Nm 22-23)? Balak was king of the Moabites, and he wanted Baalam to come and curse the Israelites for him. God, of course, wasn't going to let this happen, so while Baalam was on the way to Balak's place, God caused Baalam's donkey to stop dead in his tracks three times. Each time Baalam struck the animal, trying to get him to get moving.

Finally, when God had had enough, He allowed the donkey to voice his displeasure:

"Hey, man, get off my back! You've already put 100,000 miles on me. Don't you think by now I know what I'm doing?" (Well, those weren't the donkey's exact words, but they're close.) The donkey went on to explain to Baalam that the reason he'd stopped was because an angel of the Lord was blocking his path.

Now, let's face it, God could have spoken to Baalam through thunder. He could have had the angel tell him to quit hitting his donkey. But he allowed the donkey to speak for himself. That had to have been a pretty funny story when Baalam retold it to his friends and neighbors—after he recovered from the initial shock, that is.

I also think it must have been pretty funny when Balaam finally did arrive at Balak's place. Balak was fully expecting him to curse the Israelites, but all that comes out of Baalam's mouth was, "Hey, you guys are awesome! May you win all your battles and long be victorious!" (Or words to that effect.)

I have a feeling the Almighty must have had a pretty good laugh watching Balak's face as Balaam delivered that blessing.

That's just one story in the Bible that I feel illustrates a divine sense of humor. There are others, but the bottom line is that God created us in His image, and that includes having the ability to laugh. His Word tells us to be cheerful and live in His joy. He wants us to be happy. He enjoys the laughter of His people.

Thoughts to Ponder:

Why do you think Christians should walk in joy?

Why do you think it's healthy to laugh?

Bumper Sticker for the Day:

Laughter can turn a thirty-six-hour day back
into a twenty-four-hour day.

Scripture to Stand On:

"The cheerful heart has a continual feast." PROVERBS 15:15B

Hello Again, Lord...

Lord, Your Word says laughter is good medicine. Help
me to remember to take a healthy dose of it everyday.

Thirty-two

▲▼▲

High Hopes

Things don't always turn out the way we hope. We dream of being on the varsity team, but come down with the flu the week of tryouts. We sign up for the cheerleader competition, then sprain our ankle just before our name is called. We start out with the best of intentions, but somewhere along the line something unexpected happens.

When I start preparing dinner, I don't intend for my casserole to end up buried under three feet of dirt in the backyard. I have higher hopes for it than that (I'd envisioned only two feet).

When I begin cutting out the pattern for a new dress, I don't plan for the finished product to have one long sleeve, one short sleeve, upside-down pockets and inverted buttons. It just turns out that way.

We may make the best of plans, map out a strategy to the tiniest detail, and seemingly do everything right, yet the final outcome can still fall short of our expectations. We don't win that class presidency, make the wrestling team, or pass that SAT test.

If we don't live up to our high hopes, do we abandon them? No. We keep stretching that much more. We try a little harder next time. Our dreams may not come true today, but they may tomorrow. Or perhaps an even better dream will come true.

The world is full of people with talent they've never used or opportunities they've never taken advantage of. But a person with high hopes and the ambition to achieve them... now, there's someone who's unstoppable.

Thoughts to Ponder:

Can you think of something that didn't turn out quite as you expected?

In what way do you think you may have given up on it too easily?

How can you get back on track to achieve that goal?

Bumper Sticker for the Day:

Your plan may fall flat, but your spirit
doesn't have to fall with it.

Scripture to Stand On:

"For you have been my hope, O Sovereign Lord, my confidence since my youth."   PSALM 71:5

Hello Again, Lord...

Lord, help me to remember that my situation will never be hopeless if I've placed my hope in You.

Thirty-three
▲▼▲

One Gift—
Slightly Used

One Christmas I had only one item on my wish list—a guitar. That's all I wanted. I didn't want a new dress. I didn't want jewelry. I didn't want porcupine house slippers and glow-in-the-dark pajamas. I wanted a guitar.

I was pretty sure I was going to get it, too. After all, hadn't I been pointing it out to my mom every time we went to the store? Hadn't I posted the message on signs all over our house? Hadn't I discreetly worked it into the family dinner conversation every chance I got?

"Please pass the guitar... er, I mean, mashed potatoes."

"Mom, this is a delicious guitar... uh, meal."

"Dad, did I happen to mention I got two A's on my last guitar... I mean, report card." (I wasn't bluffing on that either. I did get two A's. Unfortunately, they were both in my name, which didn't help my grade point average any.)

Sure enough, on Christmas morning my parents presented me with a beautiful guitar.

"Do you like it?" Mom asked.

"Like it?" I shrieked. "I love it!"

I was so excited I hardly put that guitar down for the next three weeks!

After that, I hardly picked it up.

Funny how we think we can't go on without something, then once we get it, we do exactly that—go on without it. I regret now that I never learned to play the guitar. Who knows—I could have been another Wynona Judd, or maybe just a Dudd. One thing's for sure, though—I should have showed more appreciation for Mom's gift by using it.

At times I'm sure we treat a few of God's gifts the same way. We ask our heavenly Father for something, we beg and plead and pray. Then, when He gives it to us, we hardly even use it.

Thoughts to Ponder:

Has God given you a gift you're not using right now?

Why do you think you haven't used it as much as you should?

What steps can you take to start using it now?

Bumper Sticker for the Day:

Gifts are like bank accounts. They're no good if we allow ourselves to lose interest in them.

Scripture to Stand On:

"Each one should use whatever gift he has received to serve others."

1 PETER 4:10A

Hello Again, Lord...

Lord, forgive me for the times I've let Your gifts sit on the shelf collecting dust.

Thirty-four
▲ ▼ ▲

Who Am I

I wish I could tan like Carman. If I lay out on the beach all day long, the only thing I'll see turning darker is the sky.

I wish my hair was thick and beautiful like Cindy Morgan's. My hair's so thin, I can fit it all into one curler, and still have room left over.

In my opinion, Amy Grant is the perfect height. She's not too tall. When she stretches her legs out in an airplane, her feet don't hit the controls in the cockpit. I'd much rather be her size.

I wish I could sing like Point of Grace. They can break crystal with their voices. Mine just gets it thrown at me.

I wouldn't mind having eyes like Cindy Crawford, a smile like Christie Brinkley, a figure like Kim Basinger. But I don't. I've got my eyes, my smile, my voice, and my body. I'm me.

There will always be others I can compare myself to—people who are prettier or more talented than I am. But if I waste my life dwelling on the things I don't have, I'll never fully appreciate all the things I do have. I'm the only person in the world who is exactly like me. No one else has my particular talents, my particular goals. I'm the only me... and you're the only you. Each of us is one of a kind, and we're the best you and me there is.

Thoughts to Ponder:

List your best qualities or talents:

How can you make the most of those qualities or talents?

Bumper Sticker for the Day:

Life's a stage and you've got the best part—you.

Scripture to Stand On:

"But each man has his own gift from God; one has this gift, another has that." 1 CORINTHIANS 7:7B

Hello Again, Lord...

Lord, help me to strive to be the best me that I can be but to love myself like You do—just the way I am.

Thirty-five
▲▼▲

Jumping in
with Both Feet

I'm no swim instructor, but I did once teach a friend to dive. She could swim as long as her head remained above the water, but she was petrified of diving. I was petrified of diving, too. I was petrified of swimming. But I wasn't about to let her know it.

"Come on," I coaxed. "There's nothing to diving. Just hold your breath and jump into the water."

"What if I don't come back up?" she queried.

I hesitated.

"What if I don't come back up?" she repeated. "You'll jump in and save me, right?"

Jump in? I thought to myself. What is she—crazy? I can't jump in there. It's nine feet deep!

"Don't worry," I vowed. "I'll be right here to save you." That wasn't a lie either. After all, she was my best friend. I'd get her out if I had to empty the pool to do it.

She smiled and gave me that same trusting look she gave when I told her her new permanent was "just dynamite." That wasn't a lie either. If you had seen that permanent, you would have figured dynamite was involved, too.

"Go on, jump," I pressed. "You can do it."

"All right," she said, holding her breath. "Here goes." She took several determined steps along the diving board, then with one quick bounce, she was up in the air and down in the water. I had never seen such a beautiful dive before. I couldn't wait until she came up so I could tell her how impressed I was. It'd be any second now. Any second. Right about now she'd be coming up. Yessir, right about now. Just any minute now. Yep...any minute...

As I ran to dial 911, I heard her call out to me. Turning back, I saw she was on the diving board again.

"That was a blast!" she said, diving into the water once more.

I walked back to the pool and breathed a sigh of both relief and pride. I'd actually taught someone how to dive. It felt great! It felt exhilarating! It felt wonderful!

Now, if I could just learn how to swim, myself.

Thoughts to Ponder:

Is there anything in your life that your lack of confidence or your fear keeps you from doing?

What do you think is the best way to overcome that lack of confidence?

Bumper Sticker for the Day:

Changing "I can't" to "I can" is like golf.
You start by taking the "t" off.

Scripture to Stand On:

"I can do all things through Christ which strengtheneth me."

PHILIPPIANS 4:13 (KJV)

Hello Again, Lord...

Lord, help me to turn every "I can't" into a "With Your help, I can."

Thirty-six
▲ ▼ ▲

Going, Going, Gone

"They're going to give us twenty bucks for it?" I asked my sister, Melva, in disbelief. "Are you sure?"

"They said twenty," my sister repeated. "Thirty, if we throw in the old cabinet radio."

"Sold!" we exclaimed in unison, giving each other a high five. We couldn't believe what was happening. All we did was post a sign that said "Garage Sale," and our yard was swarming with shoppers. We sold the baby crib I'd long since outgrown, clothes, jewelry, dishes, antique records, whatever we could find around the house that was old and seemingly useless. Mom and Dad were away on vacation and we were determined to surprise them with more money than they could ever make in one weekend. Each time the stock on the front lawn ran low, one of us would excitedly return to the house to find more items to sell. On one trip, we weren't quick enough and a few of the customers came in after us.

"How much would you take for that two-piece sofa set?" one woman asked.

My sister and I looked at each other. It certainly wasn't new, and Mom had been talking about replacing it. Still, it was our living room furniture. If we sold it, what would the family have to sit on?

"We don't really know if we can sell that..." we hedged.

"I'll give you ten bucks for each piece," she coaxed.

Ten dollars?! That would be twenty bucks for the whole set! We had no idea how much it would cost to replace, but we did know another twenty bucks would bring our day's total to over three hundred dollars! Mom and Dad were going to be so proud of us! They were going to be thrilled! They were going to be...

"You did what?!" Mom said as she walked into the house and saw the empty spaces where furniture used to be.

"But we made over three hundred dollars!" we said, handing her the wad of bills.

"Do you have any idea what the things you sold were worth?" Her tone of voice made it hard to tell whether she was laughing or crying.

"More than three hundred dollars?" we asked meekly.

By our calculations, we can come out of our rooms in just three more years.

We learned a lot that day. And we can apply what we learned to life, integrity, and innocence. In one brief moment, we can give it all away... without even realizing its full value.

Thoughts to Ponder:

What things about you are your "valued treasures"?

What is it that makes them priceless?

Bumper Sticker of the Day:

The things you value most should never
be marked down.

Scripture to Stand On:

"Guard the good deposit that was entrusted to you—guard it
with the help of the Holy Spirit who lives in us."   2 TIMOTHY 1:14

Hello Again, Lord ...

Lord, help me to keep those things that I hold closest to my
heart closest to my heart.

Thirty-seven
▲▼▲

What a Pain!

Have you ever tried walking with a pebble in your shoe? All you had to do was remove it, but that would have taken too much time and energy. You would have had to stop, sit down, take off your shoe, remove the pebble, put your shoe back on, then stand up and start walking all over again.

Besides, it wasn't a big rock or anything. It was just a tiny pebble. So you decided to simply ignore it. You kept walking, pebble and all. Eventually, of course, you got a blister, which soon popped and almost became infected. But at least you didn't have to waste any time by stopping and removing that pebble, right?

How often do we walk around with something in our lives that shouldn't be there? We know we should get rid of it, but it's easier to ignore it and to pretend it's not there. Sure, it's affecting our walk. It's blistering, and could eventually infect the other parts of our lives, but we still choose to do nothing about it. Before long, we're complaining about the path and the pain we're forced to endure. But it's not the path that's giving us the problem. It's what we're refusing to remove.

Thoughts to Ponder:

Is there something you're having a hard time removing from your life? Explain.

Why do you think we shouldn't ignore the little things that threaten to hinder our walk?

Bumper Sticker for the Day:

Bad behaviors are like trees. They're a lot easier to remove while they're still seedlings.

Scripture to Stand On:

"Turn away from all your offenses; then sin will not be your downfall."   EZEKIEL 18:30B

Hello Again, Lord...

Lord, guide my walk. The big rocks in my path are easy to go around. It's those little ones that can really trip me up.

Thirty-eight
▲▼▲

Why Didn't You
Just Say So?

Do you have a hard time asking for what you want? I do. Even when I was young and my parents would take me to see one of those department store Santas, I'd just sit on his lap and compliment his suit.

Later, when I got to know the real Star of Christmas, I figured He had enough major problems in the world to take care of without being troubled with my little day-to-day cares.

But the Lord doesn't want us to be like that with Him. The Bible says we're to present our requests to God in prayer and with thanksgiving (see Philippians 4:6). It doesn't specify big requests or little ones. It simply says "requests."

Of course, God knows every one of our needs and desires before we even tell Him what they are. But He wants us to talk to Him about them. Even the ones we feel are insignificant.

God is a God of the lion's den, the fiery furnace, and the stormy waters. But he's also a God of the pop quiz, the job hunt, and that bruised relationship. We can take all our needs to Him—no matter what size they are.

Don't ever think your problem is too small to bother the

Lord with it. He knows about it anyway, and He might just be waiting for you to come to Him with it.

Thoughts to Ponder:

Do you talk to God about your everyday problems? How has this helped you?

Why do you think God wants us to trust Him with our small problems, too?

Bumper Sticker of the Day:

With God, all problems are small problems.

Scripture to Stand On:

"The Lord is near to all who call on Him."   PSALM 145:18A

Hello Again, Lord...

Lord, help me to realize that trusting You with my small problems helps build my faith for the big ones.

Thirty-nine
▲▼▲

Imperfectly
Perfect

I t's hard to be perfect. Just when we think we've finally attained perfection, something happens to remind us we've still got a long way to go. Others like to point out that fact, too.

We shouldn't be too hard on ourselves, though. Only one person has ever been able to lead a perfect life. That was Jesus. No one before or after Him has come close. Even those who so willingly point out our shortcomings have their own imperfections to contend with.

The good news is God doesn't expect us to be perfect. He knows we won't achieve perfection until we get to heaven. He only wants us to strive toward it, to continually improve our behavior, to daily become more Christlike.

When a mountain climber slips and slides down a few feet, he doesn't give up and walk down the rest of the mountain defeated. He just keeps right on climbing, only now he knows where not to place his foot.

When we fail, we should accept God's forgiveness and go on, vowing to do better next time. After all, why should we be harder on ourselves than God is? He forgives us for our failures. We should forgive ourselves, too.

Thoughts to Ponder:

Why do you think it's not possible for us to be perfect here on this earth?

Why is it important to strive toward perfection?

Bumper Sticker for the Day:

Sometimes the hardest person to forgive is yourself.

Scripture to Stand On:

"As far as the east is from the west, so far has he removed our transgressions from us." PSALM 103:12

Hello Again, Lord...

Lord, help me to accept Your forgiveness and live Your example.

Forty

▲▼▲

Go Ahead—
Dust Around Me

Did you know Christians aren't supposed to be lazy?

Ouch! That stings, but it really is in the Bible. In fact, the Bible mentions laziness plenty of times. I'd list all the Scriptures, but I'm too lazy (just kidding).

Romans 12:11 (KJV) says that we're to be "not slothful in business, [but] fervent in spirit; serving the Lord."

If you want to be a success at your school, on your job, and in life in general, laziness is a quality you don't want to list on your resumé. Let's face it—very few "Help Wanted" ads read:

WANTED: Laborically challenged individual who will work only when boss is looking. Hours are eight to five, but feel free to show up whenever it's convenient for you. Absolutely no enthusiasm will be tolerated. Random energy tests will be given. Those found with high levels of energy in their system will be terminated immediately. If interested, please call 555-1234 (you may wish to have someone dial it for you).

You'll probably never find an ad like that. I know. I've looked. Oddly enough, most employers want us to *earn* our paychecks. I know, I know. It sounds strange, but that's how it works.

The key to getting a job, keeping a job, and earning promotions is simple: Do what they ask you to, work hard, and get the job done. It doesn't hurt to have a positive attitude, either.

The key to better grades in school is similar. Show your teacher that you're putting forth some extra effort. Few teachers will fail a student they feel is truly trying.

As you go through life, remember—the top dog isn't the one sleeping on the porch, dreaming of Alpo-burgers. It's the one out leading the pack.

Thoughts to Ponder:
Do you feel you apply enough effort to your school or job? Why or why not?

Why do you think God doesn't want us to be lazy?

Bumper Sticker for the Day:
Resist laziness.
They bury people who stay still too long.

Scripture to Stand On:
"Lazy hands make a man poor, but diligent hands bring wealth." PROVERBS 10:4

Hello Again, Lord...
Lord, help me to remember—the more effort I give, the greater the rewards.

Forty-one
▲▼▲

Take Two

Wouldn't it be great if life were like a movie set? Every time we made a mistake, someone would simply yell, "Cut!" and we'd get to try again. "Take two!" "Take three!" "Take four!" We'd get as many tries as we'd like. It sure would save us a lot of grief, wouldn't it?

If making mistakes is how we learn, I must be an Einstein by now. But then, we've all made our share of mistakes. There are things we wish we'd done, but didn't. Things we wish we hadn't done, but did. We've said things we didn't mean to, and meant to say some things, but didn't. If we just had the chance, we know we could do the scene better next time. We'd get it right once and for all.

Sometimes we get those chances. We are able to take the words back, to right the wrongs, to make amends. Other times, it's too late. The players involved have moved on to other things and we don't know how to find them, or their departure from our life is even more permanent than that.

That's why we should be careful about the things we do and don't do, what we say and don't say. Sure, we might get a second, third, or fourth chance to make things right later. But sometimes we don't even get a "take two."

Thoughts to Ponder:

Do you have any scenes in your life story that you wish you could rewrite? Explain.

If you were given the chance, what would you do differently?

Bumper Sticker for the Day:

Some opportunities are like a good speaker.
They don't repeat themselves.

Scripture to Stand On:

"So I strive always to keep my conscience clear before God and man."   ACTS 24:16

Hello Again, Lord...

Lord, I know I might not always do and say the right thing, but when I don't, help me to right it right away.

Forty-two
▲▼▲

What a Pity!

Have you ever attended a pity party? I've thrown a few myself, and to tell you the truth, they're not a lot of fun. The refreshments leave much to be desired—sour grapes and a few lemons. And the entertainment is lousy. All you do is sit around and watch the host lick his wounds and whine to the music.

Most pity parties are BYOT (Bring Your Own Tissue), and it's best if guests RSVP. (Really Sob Very Pathetically).

A few games might be played—like "Pin the Pity on the Hostess" or "Sympathy Charades."

The problem with pity parties, though, is that guests never want to stay very long. While friends and family may drop by for a few minutes, once they realize it's a pity party they start making excuses to leave. The host, on the other hand, is ready to party all night.

The next time you think about throwing a pity party for yourself, remember—you just might be the only one attending. And when you get right down to it, is that any way to have a party?

Thoughts to Ponder:

Have you ever thrown a pity party for yourself or attended someone else's? Tell about it.

Why do you think pity parties aren't any fun for the guests?

Do you think the person throwing the pity party is having any real fun? Why or why not?

Bumper Sticker for the Day:

It's a fact—no one crashes a pity party.

Scripture to Stand On:

"I am greatly encouraged; in all our troubles my joy knows no bounds."   2 CORINTHIANS 7:4

Hello Again, Lord...

Lord, help me to remember that when I hold a pity party, I'm the one missing out on all the fun.

Forty-three
▲ ▼ ▲

Flight Patterns

The shortest distance between two points is a straight line, but we sometimes choose to take a different route.

On a recent trip to Nashville, Tennessee, I could have selected the comfortable, nonstop flight I usually take, but decided to save a little money instead. I booked myself with one of those "no frills" airlines where the only safety speech they give you is, "I'd get off this plane right now if I were you."

My flight was scheduled to depart from Los Angeles International Airport at 8:00 a.m. Figuring I'd have breakfast in flight, I skipped my morning nutrition and rushed to the airport. I soon discovered, however, that "no frills" also means "no food" except peanuts and water. (No wonder elephants never forget. If that's all you got to eat, you wouldn't forget it, either!)

I'll eat when we change planes in St. Louis, I thought to myself while my stomach growled louder than the engines.

But instead of landing in St. Louis, we were rerouted north to Dallas due to bad weather. (Evidently, there was a slight breeze blowing and the pilot didn't want to lose another one of the wings.)

After landing in Dallas, I had to rush to catch my connecting flight. Only they didn't have any flights going straight to Nashville. I'd have to fly south to Houston, before catching another flight back up north to Nashville. Somehow, all this rerouting was saving the airline money, and since they'd given me such a good price on my ticket, I couldn't complain, right?

I didn't get to Nashville until after 8:00 that evening. That was twelve hours, nine sodas and fourteen miniature bags of peanuts later.

Sometimes we choose the long route in our lives, too. There's a simple, straightforward way to get where we're going, but we refuse to take it. We go completely out of our way, take twice as long to reach our destination, and have a miserable time in the process.

Maybe it's time we got back on God's course.

Thoughts to Ponder:

List one of your goals in life:

Is the path you're taking to achieve that goal the straightest one, or are you making a lot of detours?

What can you do to make sure you're on the course that God has planned for you?

Bumper Sticker of the Day:

You can either walk across the street directly or go all the way around the world. It all depends on which route you take.

Scripture to Stand On:

"Teach me your way, O Lord; lead me in a straight path."

PSALM 27:11A

Hello Again, Lord...

Lord, help me to remember that the course You've planned for my life will always be the best one to take.

Forty-four

▲▼▲

Explode Mode

O ver the years I've seen my meat-loaf and my turkey explode; I've even seen a few *people* explode—their tempers, anyway.

Do you ever get mad? Silly question, huh? We all get angry from time to time. And that's okay. The Bible does say, however, that we should be careful not to sin in our anger (Eph 4:26).

Have you ever watched people go ballistic over something? You might say they "lost it"—they lost their patience, or their temper, but most importantly, they may have lost some of their Christian witness.

Sure, it's all right to let off a little steam every so often. It may even be healthy. But we need to be careful that when we do, we don't burn ourselves or someone else in the process.

The Bible says that God is "slow to anger, abounding in love and faithfulness" (Ps 86:15b). We should be, too. Being slow to anger gives us a chance to collect our thoughts, and make sure we don't say or do something we'll regret. After all, bitter words spoken in anger may have to be eaten later. So, make sure it's just a snack. Not a seven-course meal.

Thoughts to Ponder:

Have you ever said something in anger that you later came to regret? Explain.

✎

Why do you think it's important for a Christian to control his or her temper?

✎

Bumper Sticker for the Day:

People who are always hot under the collar
only burn themselves.

Scripture to Stand On:

"A fool gives full vent to his anger, but a wise man keeps himself under control." PROVERBS 29:11

Hello Again, Lord...

Lord, help me to remember that if I keep blowing gaskets, I won't have much of an engine left.

Forty-five
▲ ▼ ▲

A Change
of Face

Do you put on a smiling face in front of others, then take it off when you're alone? Is there a face you wear with your friends, and another one you wear with your family?

On Sundays, do you put on your church face, then change to a completely different one for the rest of the week?

When you're feeling down, do you put on a false front of joy for everyone else?

Some of us have a different face for every occasion, situation and group we happen to encounter. But we're only fooling ourselves.

We can think we're hiding our pain behind that smile, or hiding our faults behind that pious expression, but God knows the truth. We can't fool Him. He can see through every facade, every mask, every false front we try to put on. He knows when we're faking happiness or pretending to be someone we're not. He sees the person we are on Friday night, as well as the person we are on Sunday morning.

God sees our weaknesses, not just our cover-ups. He can see through every one of our faces because He can see through to the heart.

Thoughts to Ponder:

Do you find yourself wearing different faces for different people? Why?

Why do you think God is more interested in the condition of your heart, rather than the expression on your face?

Bumper Sticker of the Day:

If God wanted us to have two faces, He would have redesigned Adam and Eve.

Scripture to Stand On:

"As water reflects a face, so a man's heart reflects the man."

PROVERBS 27:19

Hello Again, Lord...

Lord, help me to realize that goodness and joy are more than skin deep.

Forty-Six

▲▼▲

Worried Sick

Did you know that most of what we worry about will never happen? Why, then, do we worry?

Good question.

I've known people who worried about not getting a job, then they worried about the job they got. They worried about failing their driving test, then they worried about driving once they passed the test. Some even seem to worry about running out of things to worry about.

Not only is worrying unhealthy, it's unnecessary. The Bible tells us we shouldn't worry about the future. Jesus says, "Therefore do not worry about tomorrow, for tomorrow will worry about itself. Each day has enough trouble of its own" (Mt 6:34).

Now that doesn't mean we're to use that verse to show our parents why we don't have to do our chores tomorrow or go on that job interview next week. (We can try it, but it won't get us anywhere because the Bible also has plenty of verses concerning laziness, which many Christian parents can quote by heart!)

Jesus is saying we're not to fret over the uncertainties of this life. If our hearts are full of faith, there won't be any room for worry. Put simply, we're to take care of the things we can, and leave the rest to God.

Thoughts to Ponder:

Write about a time you worried about something that never happened.

Do you think worrying about it did any good?

Why or why not?

What should you have done instead of worrying?

Bumper Sticker of the Day:
Worry won't put a wrinkle in your problem.
Only on your face.

Scripture to Stand On:
"Who of you by worrying can add a single hour to his life?"

MATTHEW 6:27

Hello Again, Lord...
Lord, I have no need to worry, for You love me and are in control of everything that comes my way.

Forty-seven

▲▼▲

Living Loud

Would you have much confidence in an exercise coach who barked out each step of a routine while lying on a hammock eating chocolate chip cookies and Klondike Bars? Would you listen as someone who's fifty-five and still riding a skateboard to work tells you of his latest get-rich-quick schemes?

Who'd listen to a marriage counselor who was on his fourth marriage, or a speech teacher who mumbled? It'd be hard to trust a dentist who had only four decayed teeth left, or to respect a doctor who chain-smoked and ate butter-on-a-stick for lunch every day.

Most of us would agree: the messenger should live the message.

This is especially true when it comes to being a Christian. Some people can talk Christianity beautifully. They say all the right things, quote all the correct biblical passages, point out exactly what this one needs in her life and what that one needs in his life. But it's hard to believe what they're saying, though, when they're walking so loudly in the opposite direction.

We can shout our message, scream it, yell it from the housetops, but if our life doesn't back it up, what good is all that volume?

In other words, the best testimony we can give is the one we live.

Thoughts to Ponder:

Why do you think it's so important that our talk be consistent with our walk?

✎

Do you think your friends watch how you live your life? What do they see?

✎

Bumper Sticker of the Day:

Talking may be easier,
but walking will get you a lot farther.

Scripture to Stand On:

"Whoever claims to live in Him must walk as Jesus did."

1 JOHN 2:6

Hello Again, Lord...

Lord, help my walk to always keep pace with my talk.

Forty-eight
▲ ▼ ▲

Lean on Me...
for a While

"**O**w!" I screamed.

Limping off the volleyball court, I sat down in a nearby grassy area. I could feel my ankle swelling as the PE teacher placed an ice pack on it.

"You'd better get this checked," she said, then handed me a pass to the office. The nurse called my mother, who left work and drove me to the doctor.

My ankle throbbed the entire way there, but an x-ray soon revealed the good news: I hadn't broken any bones. I just had a bad sprain.

"I still recommend that you stay off it," my doctor said. "Do you have any crutches at home?"

My mother assured him we did and made me vow to use them.

The crutches really helped. They kept the weight off my foot and promoted rapid healing. Almost too rapid. Within days, the swelling had subsided, the color had returned to normal, and the pain was gone.

The crutches took longer to go away. I had grown used to them... and what they could get me. They got me out of class five minutes ahead of everyone else. They got me to the front of the cafeteria line. They got me into lots of conversations I wouldn't have had otherwise. People asked about my accident, about my x-rays, about me. Those crutches had become... well, they had become a crutch.

A person can have other kinds of crutches besides the metal or wooden ones. Sometimes a crutch can be a friend, a fear, a bad habit, whatever we use as an excuse to keep from standing on our own.

"I really want to be in that play, but I'm afraid."

"I wish I could be a drummer in a band, but between my friends and my favorite television shows, when would I have time to practice?"

"I'd quit cheating on my homework, but then I wouldn't pass history."

These crutches help us rationalize why we can't be all we could be, why we hold back from going after goals or achieving things we're capable of achieving. Such crutches hinder more than they help.

Thoughts to Ponder:

What might you be using as a "crutch"?

What are you allowing it to keep you from doing? Why?

Bumper Sticker for the Day:
That which we think is holding us up
may be what's keeping us from standing.

Scripture to Stand On:

"And he will stand, for the Lord is able to make him stand."

Hello Again, Lord...

Lord, when I need to lean, let it be on You.

Forty-nine
▲▼▲

Now That
Makes Scents

Have you ever tried to locate the source of a strange and foul odor that has been emanating from somewhere in your bedroom? A quick glance under your bed discloses a three-week-old pizza, two petrified doughnuts and a banana that's grown its own dreadlocks, but they're not responsible for that rank odor. They're responsible for a different rank odor, but not the one that's melting the glue from your wallpaper.

A few more whiffs lead you in the direction of your closet. As you open the door, the odor becomes so strong it takes the perm out of your hair, so you know you're hot on the trail. You look through your sports equipment. Nothing. You look behind your videotape collection. Nothing. You look inside the shoe boxes. Still nothing.

As you start checking through your clothes, you notice the odor growing even stronger. It's not coming from your jackets. It's not coming from your sweaters. It's coming from your bathrobe. It's coming from the pocket of your bathrobe. It's coming from the colored egg in the pocket of your bathrobe.

Now you remember. This was that lone egg no one could find at last year's Easter egg hunt. Or was it the Easter before that? Or the Easter before that?

Sin can be like that egg, you know. We can hide it away, we can think no one else will notice it, we can pretend it's not there, but sooner or later it'll start smelling up our lives. We need to get rid of it. The Bible says all we have to do is confess our sins and God is faithful and just to forgive us of each and every one of them (1 Jn 1:9). So why hold your nose a minute longer? Get rid of those rotten eggs... and breathe happily ever after.

Thoughts to Ponder:

Why do you suppose some people insist on hanging on to behaviors they know are sinful and not pleasing to the Lord?

Have you ever tried hiding a part of your heart from God? If so, how successful did you feel?

Bumper Sticker for the Day:

It's a lot easier to go through life with your heart cleansed than with your nose plugged.

Scripture to Stand On:

"The Lord does not look at the things man looks at. Man looks at the outward appearance, but the Lord looks at the heart."

1 SAMUEL 16:7B

Hello Again, Lord...

Forgive me, Lord, of all my sins... even the ones I thought I'd hid from You.

Fifty
▲▼▲

Where's
the Fire?

Sometimes I think life should come with speedbumps. It can get hectic. We rush to this, we race to that, we hardly have a moment to spare. Every so often we need to tap the brakes and slow down our pace.

Life hasn't always been this way. Adam and Eve didn't have to keep appointment calendars. Moses didn't have a beeper or cellular phone—and look how many people he was in charge of. Noah didn't buy an E-Z Assembly Ark kit because he was already working overtime at the office and could spare only so much time for God's work.

The pace was much slower back then. People didn't cook in microwave ovens, use speed dialing to call their friends, or add rocket boosters to their chariots to make them go faster. Of course, none of those things were invented yet—but sometimes I wonder if progress hasn't speeded up life more than we wanted it to.

I'm not saying that our modern conveniences are bad. It's just that from time to time we need to slow down and take in a little more of the scenery. After all, if we're always fast-forwarding through this life, we could be missing the opportunity to make a difference in it.

Thoughts to Ponder:

Do you ever feel like you're moving too fast? Explain.

✎

What can you do to make sure you allow enough time for God?

✎

Bumper Sticker of the Day:

Racing through life will only get you
to the finish line that much faster.

Scripture to Stand On:

"Be still before the Lord and wait patiently for him." PSALM 37:7A

Hello Again, Lord...

Lord, keep me from becoming so busy that I don't make time for You.

Fifty-one
▲▼▲

See You
in the Morning

Sometimes things come up that get us down. We see no way out. The situation looks hopeless. What should we do at times like these?

Wait on the Lord.

Most of us know how to pray. We're good at sharing our feelings with our heavenly Father. Waiting on Him is harder to do. We want our problem solved now, immediately, pronto. We don't want to wait.

But waiting can teach us important things such as faith, patience and endurance. How many times have you given up on something minutes too soon? That telephone call you were expecting came right after you walked out the door. That jacket went on sale the day after you paid full price for it. That person you were waiting for showed up less than five minutes after you left.

The answers to our problems can come the same way—right after we give up. But we get impatient. We think the answer has to come today, but God knows when we really need it. So wait. No matter how dark the night, morning is always just around the corner.

Thoughts to Ponder:

Have you ever been in a situation that seemed hopeless but wasn't? What was it?

What can you learn from waiting on the Lord?

Bumper Sticker for the Day:

When you get to the end of your rope, look up. You could be at the end that's tied to the rock.

Scripture to Stand On:

"But they that wait upon the Lord shall renew their strength; they shall mount up with wings as eagles; they shall run and not be weary; and they shall walk, and not faint."

ISAIAH 40:31 (KJV)

Hello Again, Lord...

Lord, help me with my "wait" problem, for I know You'll see me through whatever comes my way.

Fifty-two
▲▼▲

That Ought to
Teach You a Lesson

L ife can teach us a lot of lessons. Some we have to learn for ourselves, others we can learn from someone else's experience... if we're smart.

Our parents have learned their share of lessons. When my father was young, he played a prank on his teacher by sneaking a cow into his second-story classroom. My dad told me how hard it was to get the cow to walk up the stairs (I guess she'd heard about that teacher, too). Dad also told about the punishment he received for pulling such a prank. I don't have to repeat that gag to learn the lessons he learned from it. By accepting his word for it, I know for a fact that it's better to buy milk at school than to bring in the whole cow.

Our uncles, aunts, grandmothers, grandfathers, pastors and youth ministers have all learned lessons as well. Instead of tuning them out, we could learn a great deal by tuning them in. Growing through someone else's experience can save us a lot of trouble and grief.

We don't have to reenact Jonah's adventure and spend three days in the belly of a whale before we accept that running from God doesn't pay. When Jonah advises that it's better to be obedient than to be a whale appetizer, we don't have to test the theory.

We don't have to fly a kite with a key attached to it to learn what Benjamin Franklin learned—that lightning could strike it, creating electricity (and also giving us the "mother of all perms"!)

No one can (or should) learn all of life's lessons from a first-hand experience. After all, sometimes the things we don't do are just as important as the things we do.

Thoughts to Ponder:

What's the most important lesson you've learned from someone else's experience?

What's a good lesson you've learned from your own experiences that you could share with someone else?

Bumper Sticker of the Day:

Every experience has a lesson, but every lesson doesn't have to have an experience.

Scripture to Stand On:

"Apply your heart to instruction and your ears to words of knowledge." PROVERBS 23:12

Hello Again, Lord...

Lord, help me to remember that as long as I'm teachable, I'm reachable.

Fifty-three
▲▼▲

Help! I've Fallen and I Can't Get Up!

We all know what it feels like to fall. But falling down doesn't mean we're out of the game.

Look at any sporting event. A player falls, the crowd gasps, tension fills the air. Then, after a few nervous moments, he rises to his feet and the crowd goes wild. He's back in the game and everyone's rooting for him.

Only when a player doesn't get up does the situation become tragic.

None of us want to fail. We want to do the right thing, make good judgment calls, pass those tests of our faith with flying colors. We have the best of intentions, yet we can still fall flat on our faces.

What's our next move? Do we just lie there on the field waiting for some three-hundred-pound linebacker to drop-kick us into the locker room? Of course not.

In 1 Samuel 13:14 David was called "a man after God's own heart." After he committed sin with Bathsheba (see 2 Samuel 11), he could have given up in shame. But he didn't. He asked forgiveness and continued to serve God.

Moses could have felt worthless after he committed murder (Ex 2:11-12). But he repented and God was still able to use him.

It's not always easy to make the right decisions. When we

make wrong ones and fall, getting up can seem pretty difficult. We can feel defeated, embarrassed, hopeless. But the situation isn't hopeless. We may have fallen, but with God's help, we can get up.

Thoughts to Ponder:

Have you ever had a hard time getting back up on your feet after a fall? What happened?

✎

What held you back?

✎

What could you have done differently to get back on your feet?

✎

Bumper Sticker for the Day:

Sometimes we're on the bench because
we've taken ourselves out of the game.

Scripture to Stand On:

"[I am] confident of this, that he who began a good work in you will carry it on to completion, until the day of Christ Jesus." PHILIPPIANS 1:6

Hello Again, Lord...

Lord, You never give up on me. Help me not to give up on myself.

Fifty-four
▲▼▲

Knock, Knock

No, I wasn't dreaming. I was at a party with former President of the United States Ronald Reagan. I knew none of my friends were going to believe this, so I had to try to capture this Kodak moment on film.

I handed the camera to my husband, and, for the rest of the evening, discreetly tried to situate myself near Mr. Reagan. I figured if I could just get close to him, the picture might appear as though we were actually conversing.

When he walked by the refreshment table, I maneuvered my way behind him along with twenty other like-minded people, and got lost in the crowd. I waited for the president to sit down, then nonchalantly strolled by his table. That would have been a great shot, too, but his back was to the camera.

Finally, I got up the courage to just ask,

"Mr. President, would you mind taking a picture with me?"

"I'd be happy to," he smiled.

I couldn't believe it! Here was the fortieth President of the United States standing next to me, posing for a picture. It was the opportunity of a lifetime. I flashed a big smile. He flashed a big smile. Unfortunately, the *flash* didn't flash.

My heart sank. There went my chance of a lifetime.

"Would you like to try it again?" Mr. Reagan said. Again? A president of the United States was willing to stand there while I tried it *again?* What a nice man, I thought. So, once more I smiled. Once more he smiled. Once more the flash didn't do a thing.

There was nothing left for me to do but apologize. He shook my hand, said a few warm words, then continued mingling with the other guests. Needless to say, the next morning I went out and bought a new camera. But my big moment was gone.

When opportunity knocks, we can't tell it to come back next week when we're better prepared. Certain opportunities may only come our way once. Like the Bible says, we need to be prepared in season and out of season (see 2 Timothy 4:2).

Thoughts to Ponder:

Have you ever missed out on an opportunity because you weren't prepared? What was it?

Why do you think God wants us to be prepared for opportunities that may come our way?

Bumper Sticker for the Day:

Opportunities can be like some waiters. They come around once, then you never see them again.

Scripture to Stand On:

"Always be prepared to give an answer to everyone who asks you to give the reason for the hope you have."   1 Peter 3:15b

Hello Again, Lord...

Lord, when opportunity knocks, help me to be ready to answer the door.

Fifty-five
▲▼▲

If I Only
Had a Brain

I did some pretty foolish things when I was growing up. I'd naïvely place myself in dangerous situations, then pray for God to rescue me. I'd hike in places where the scoutleader told me not to. I'd climb trees that were too high, then scream for help. I knew all the city fire and rescue workers even before I cooked my first meal.

When God gave us our brains, He didn't mean for us to merely carry them around until we reached adulthood. He intended for us to begin using them right away... so we can *reach* adulthood.

Our brain gives us common sense. It's what tells us when we're doing something unsafe. We should listen to it.

Common sense tells us not to approach a sleeping bear, unless our goal in life is to become a Camper McNugget. Common sense tells us not to hike Mount McKinley with just a lunchbox of Ding Dongs. (A hike like that requires at least two lunchboxes of Ding Dongs and the phone number of the local Domino's.) And common sense tells us not to surf in toxic waste. Not only will the sludge slow down our board, but glowing for the next two weeks might really annoy our friends.

Sure, God gave us a free will to do whatever we wish. But

He also gave us a brain. I've found life goes so much easier if we use them both at the same time.

Thoughts to Ponder:

Have you ever placed yourself in jeopardy? How?

Looking back on it now, was it worth the risk it posed to your health or safety? Why or why not?

Why do you think God gave us common sense?

Bumper Sticker for the Day:

Doing the right thing usually means
doing the smart thing, too.

Scripture to Stand On:

"For the Lord gives wisdom, and from his mouth come knowledge and understanding."   PROVERBS 2:6

Hello Again, Lord...

Lord, give me Your wisdom in the choices I make each day.

Fifty-six
▲▼▲

A "Trying" Experience

"I can't do it!"

Sound familiar? Has fear of failure ever kept you from doing something you really wanted to do? Perhaps you were scheduled to sing a solo, but decided you couldn't go through with it and didn't show up. (I was scheduled to sing a solo once, and the audience said they couldn't go through with it and didn't show up!)

Maybe you wanted to try out for that part in the school play, but ended up talking yourself out of it. "What if I don't get the part?" "What if I do get the part and forget my lines?" "What if I remember every single line perfectly, then find out I studied the wrong script?"

Remember when you were little and your mother or father would coax you into sampling new food items? "Just try it," they'd say. Some of the items were good, some of them made you gag. That's how you found out which ones were which. By trying.

That's also how we find out where our talents lie—by trying. Failure isn't hitting the wrong notes or forgetting your lines in a play. Putting forth your best effort and following through with something is success in itself. It's only when we don't try that we've truly failed.

Thoughts to Ponder:

Why do you think we fear failure so much?

What are you letting fear keep you from trying?

Bumper Sticker of the Day:

If at first you don't succeed, you've got something
to look forward to tomorrow.

Scripture to Stand On:

"I sought the Lord, and he answered me; he delivered me
from all my fears."   PSALM 34:4

Hello Again, Lord...

Lord, help me to always be willing to try.

Fifty-seven

▲ ▼ ▲

Repeat Offense

Some sins are easy to overcome. We commit them once, learn our lesson, and never even think of repeating them. Others may be a little harder to resist. They're like a certain brand of potato chip. We can't stop with just one handful. We've got to keep going back for another sample, and another, and another.

Maybe you have a particular sin you're struggling with. No matter how hard you work at overcoming it, you just can't seem to stop doing it. You wish you weren't so weak. You wish you could stand up to that sin the way you have done to so many others. But you can't.

Or can you? Did you know the Bible promises that we'll never be tempted more than we can bear? And when we are tempted, it tells us that God will provide a way out for us.

"No temptation has seized you except what is common to man. And God is faithful; he will not let you be tempted beyond what you can bear. But when you are tempted, he will also provide a way out so that you can stand up under it" (1 Cor 10:13).

The next time we get to feeling that a sin is bigger than we are, we need to stop and look again. God has already given us the strength to stand up to it. It's up to us to just say no.

Thoughts to Ponder:

Why do you think some sins are harder for us to resist than others?

✎

What should we do to help ourselves resist temptation when it comes?

✎

Bumper Sticker for the Day:

"No" is one of the first words we learn in this life.
It shouldn't be one of the first we forget.

Scripture to Stand On:

"Because he himself suffered when he was tempted, he is able to help those who are being tempted." HEBREWS 2:18

Hello Again, Lord...

Lord, help me to say "no" to those things I shouldn't do, and "yes" to those I should do.

Fifty-eight
▲▼▲

In Last Place

When I was young, my pastor put together a promotional contest to attract people to Sunday School. He mailed every family on the church mailing list an envelope of paper keys. The keys were different colors, and there was one for each family member. The accompanying letter stated that one of the keys was a "special" key which could be traded in on Sunday morning for a prize.

Since I was the one in my family to open the envelope, I had first choice of the keys. Was the blue key the special one? Or was it the red one? Or the green one? I couldn't decide, so I did something scriptural without realizing it. I let everyone else make their selections and I took what was left.

Unfortunately, what was left was the goldenrod key. "Goldenrod" is a mix between yellow and gold. To my eye it didn't look very prize-worthy, but I was stuck with it. There was no one to blame but myself.

When we arrived at church on Sunday, you could sense the excitement. Everyone had their keys and anxiously awaited the pastor's announcement. About halfway through the service, it finally came.

"The special key color is...," he paused for just a moment. "The special color is... goldenrod."

Goldenrod? I couldn't believe it. What's so special about goldenrod? I didn't debate the issue any more than that.

Instead, I walked up on stage with the other winners and received my free gift. It was a plaque that said "God Answers Prayer."

To this day, that plaque hangs over my bed, reminding me of two very important truths—God indeed answers prayer, and it really does pay to put yourself last.

Thoughts to Ponder:

Why do you think it's better for us to put ourselves last rather than first?

What do you think Jesus meant when He said in Matthew 20:16 that the last will be first and the first will be last?

Bumper Sticker for the Day:

When you start out last, everything from then on is a promotion.

Scripture to Stand On:

"Humble yourselves before the Lord, and He will lift you up."

JAMES 4:10

Hello Again, Lord...

Lord, help me to remember that when I put myself last, I win by a mile.

Fifty-nine
▲▼▲

Living
on the Edge

I don't like living life on the edge—the edge of anything.

I never lean against the railings on balconies, stand on the edges of cliffs, or drive in the outside lane over bridges. Whenever I visit the Grand Canyon, I try to stand as far away from the rim as possible—like maybe in Idaho. I prefer knowing there's plenty of space between me and any drop of more than two feet. After all, if I stand too close to the edge, I might accidentally slip and take up bungee jumping without a bungee.

As Christians, we can sometimes stand too close to the edge. We wander off the path of safety and get dangerously close to behaviors we shouldn't participate in. We might even lean over God's safety railings from time to time and do our own thing, regardless of the warnings He's posted against it.

Wouldn't it be better to walk as far away from the edge as we can? Back to where our footing is more steady. Back to where the terrain is solid and dependable. Back to where if we slip and fall, all we have to do is stand back up... instead of climbing the whole mountain again.

Thoughts to Ponder:

Have you found yourself living life close to the edge? Explain.

Why do you think it's important that we, as Christians, walk far away from compromise?

Bumper Sticker for the Day:

A cliff is only a threat to those who are trying to balance themselves on the edge of it.

Scripture to Stand On:

"Can a man scoop fire into his lap without his clothes being burned? Can a man walk on hot coals without his feet being scorched?"   PROVERBS 6:27-28

Hello Again, Lord...

Lord, help me to stay on Your path where my footsteps are secure.

Sixty

▲▼▲

The Alone Zone

Have you ever been lonely? Not alone. Lonely. There's a difference.

I've spent my share of time alone. I've been surrounded by crowds of people only to have them all disappear the minute I said, "Dinner's ready." I've hit the first notes of my solo, then looked around the church and found myself alone once again. The choir was gone, the musicians had disappeared, even the congregation had vanished. I was left standing on stage all by myself wondering if the Lord had come back and I didn't hear the trumpet sound over my high C.

Loneliness, though, has little to do with being alone. It's about feeling emotionally apart from others. Some people can be by themselves and never once feel lonely, while others can be in a crowded room and feel like the loneliest people on earth.

I know I never have to feel lonely because God has promised in His Word never to leave me. Psalm 73:23 tells me that He's always with me and holds me by my right hand. Yes, in that empty sanctuary with no one to hear my solo except the mice (and even they've boarded up their mouse holes), God is with me. When I'm the only brave soul willing to stick around and try my stuffed tuna towers with chocolate mushroom sauce, God is there with me. (Not only is He with me, but He might even assign a few more angels to watch over me that night!)

Whether you're all by yourself in your room or watching a football game with a stadium full of people, if you suddenly start feeling lonely, just remember, the best friend you could ever have is as close as your heart.

Thoughts to Ponder:

Why do you think some people feel lonely when they are in a crowd?

Have you ever felt lonely? When?

If God's Word says He'll always be with us, are we ever really alone? How does this make you feel?

Bumper Sticker for the Day:

With God, you're always a party of two.

Scripture to Stand On:

"Never will I leave you; never will I forsake you."   HEBREWS 13:5B

Hello Again, Lord...

Thank You, Lord, for being the kind of friend who stays when others leave.

Part Three
▲▼▲

Follow the Leader

This is the final section. It's also the most important. It deals with our relationship with the Lord. If this relationship is in proper working order, it will help all our other relationships fall into place.

(Can you believe it? Sixty chapters so far and I haven't given out a single *one* of my recipes!)

Sixty-one

▲ ▼ ▲

Staying
in Our Place

They sell a product in California called "Quake Wax." You place it on the bottom of an object and it's supposed to keep it in place in the middle of an earthquake. Museums use a lot of Quake Wax. It keeps their statues from breakdancing together during a six pointer.

Frankly, I'm impressed with the product and would like to order about four cases of it. I'd put it on everything I don't want falling—my living room lamps, my paintings, my savings account balance.

I can think of a lot of other good uses for it, too. During league finals in basketball, we could put it on the soles of the opposing team's shoes. Then, when they try to go up for a slam dunk, their Air Jordans would become Floor Jordans and give our team just the edge we need. And think how much easier babysitting would be if we could get the kids to sit down in a pile of it. We wouldn't have to worry about them for the rest of the evening.

The uses for Quake Wax could be unlimited. But what really would be terrific is some "Faith Wax"—something to keep our faith intact when everything is shaking around us.

Fortunately, God has given us all the Faith Wax we'll ever need. It's called His Word. It's up to us to dab a little around our lives everyday.

Thoughts to Ponder:

Describe a trial or test you've had to deal with recently.

How did you react to it?

What advice or assurance can you find in God's Word that could help you deal with a similar situation in the future?

Bumper Sticker for the Day:

Faith should be like rock salt—unshakable.

Scripture to Stand On:

"Those who trust in the Lord are like Mount Zion, which cannot be shaken but endures forever."   PSALMS 125:1

Hello Again, Lord ...

Lord, thank You for Your Word, for it is my stabilizer in an unstable world.

Sixty-two
▲▼▲

The Gratitude
Attitude

How would you feel if you gave someone a beautiful bouquet of flowers every single day and never once heard a thank-you? What if you fed, clothed, and provided shelter for someone, and still received not a single word of gratitude?

Most of us would be offended. Some of us would tell that person to eat dirt hoagies and dress in shrubbery for all we care. After all, people who can't manage to voice a simple thank-you should be left to fend for themselves, right?

As children, we're taught to be grateful for what we've been given. When we open that Christmas gift—you know, the T-shirt with the flashing neon lights that spell out "My Aunt Ola Loves Me"—we're to smile and say thanks. When we get those hand-crocheted booties from Grandma Sarah (the ones that stretch up to our necks), we're expected to jump up and give her a big hug and kiss just to show our gratitude.

That's what we're taught to do and that's what we should do. But how many days do we let go by without taking the time to thank our heavenly Father for the many blessings He gives us?

We really do take a lot for granted. The Lord provides food for us to eat, water for us to drink, and brings us flowers every day; yet sometimes we ignore Him as if He's not even there.

But He is there. He's always there. And He deserves our thanks.

One of my favorite stories in the Bible is about the ten lepers (see Luke 17:11-19). What a lesson in common manners! Jesus healed all ten lepers of their incurable disease, yet only one had the courtesy to return and say thanks. Can you believe that? Their ugly sores fell off, their skin became as smooth as a newborn baby's, but evidently they had better things to do than show their gratitude.

God didn't withdraw His miracle of healing from the nine, but He did feel it was important enough to mention in His Word that only one returned to express any thankfulness. God wants us to be grateful. He likes to know we appreciate His goodness.

So before we start enjoying tomorrow's blessings, perhaps we should pause and give thanks for today's.

Thoughts to Ponder:

Why do you think it's important to thank someone for the things they do for you?

Can you think of some things that you need to thank God for?

Bumper Sticker for the Day:

Always take time to stop and smell the roses... and thank the One who made them.

Scripture to Stand On:

"Give thanks to the Lord, for He is good."   PSALM 118:1A

Hello Again, Lord ...

Lord, help me to show my gratitude on a daily basis, for that's how often Your blessings come.

Sixty-three

▲▼▲

Hangin' in There

Picture this: You drive to your local mini-mart for some ice cream, but it's closed. The neon sign on top of the building says "Open 24 hours," but the doors are locked, the lights have been turned out, no one's there. Upon closer inspection you notice a sign in the window that reads, "Tired. Gone home."

An hour later (after you've gone someplace else to get your double scoop of Chocolate Ecstasy) you drive by the mini-mart again. Now the sign reads, "Feeling better. Come on in." You could go for some chocolate chip cookies right about now, so you decide to stop. Before you can park and get out of your car, however, the store manager changes the sign again. Just as the lights of the building are going off, you manage to read it. It says, "Feeling great now. Gone fishing!"

It wouldn't be easy shopping at a store like that, would it? If a market advertises that it's going to be open twenty-four hours, it should stay open twenty-four hours. We want the hours to be dependable. We want to be able to shop whenever we need to. We want a place we can count on. We want consistency.

God is consistent. He promises to be there twenty-four hours a day, seven days a week. When we need Him, He won't say, "Sorry, but I'm feeling a little weary today. Find someone else to take care of your needs."

As far as I can tell, God hasn't taken a day off since the seventh day of creation. He's *always* there for His children.

It's important for us to be consistent, too. God has work for us to do. What good are we if we're open to His call today, but closed to it tomorrow? Or if we're here for Him in the morning hours, but our hearts have "gone fishing" by midafternoon?

God needs us to be people He can count on every day, all day. Just like we can count on Him.

Thoughts to Ponder:

Why do you think consistency is so important in our Christian walk?

What comfort do you have in knowing that the Lord will always be there for you?

Bumper Sticker for the Day:

Only snowmen have an excuse for "flaking out."

Scripture to Stand On:

"Jesus Christ is the same yesterday and today and forever."

HEBREWS 13:8

Hello Again, Lord...

Lord, consistency is one of Your best qualities. Help me to make it one of mine.

Sixty-four

▲▼▲

In the
Driver's Seat

I t took four tries to get my driver's license. I probably shouldn't have passed the test at all, but it was the only way the examiners at the Department of Motor Vehicles could be assured they wouldn't have to get into a car with me again.

Driving an automobile isn't easy. There are rules to follow. You have to deal with a lot of emergency situations, unexpected road conditions, and police officers who don't appreciate your triple U-turns while you decide which way you want to go. You have to watch out for those other drivers on the road, too.

Living the Christian life can be a lot like driving a car. There might be days when we just can't seem to get started, and other days when we go and go and go until we overheat and have to pull to the side of the road and rest awhile.

In our enthusiasm, we may run a few of God's stop signs or fail to heed His caution lights. We may stay parked long after He's given us a green light, or be so eager to please others that we don't yield the right-of-way to our own convictions.

God posts His road signs for a reason. When we come to one of His caution lights, we should slow down. There might be a road hazard just around the corner that only He can see.

We shouldn't hesitate at His green lights either. There could be something wonderful waiting for us down the road, but we'll never know until we shift into gear and get moving.

Yes, God has mapped out the perfect journey for us. His road signs will lead and guide us. But we're the ones in the driver's seat. It's up to us to follow His directions.

Thoughts to Ponder:

Why do you think God sometimes puts stop signs in our path?

Why is it important to heed God's direction as we travel through this life?

Bumper Sticker for the Day:

Sometimes it isn't the road that's treacherous.
It's our driving.

Scripture to Stand On:

"I will instruct you and teach you in the way you should go."

PSALM 32:8A

Hello Again, Lord...

Lord, help me to trust in Your guidance... especially around the blind curves.

Sixty-five

▲▼▲

You Can
Bank on It

Do you have a hard time saving money? You fully intended to deposit some of your babysitting cash into your savings account, but on the way to the bank you drove by Foot Locker and just had to stop for a new pair of hightops. After that you found yourself in the drive-through at Burger King, which, oddly enough, funneled you right into the parking lot of Macy's department store where they were having a huge summer fashion clearance.

By the time you got to the bank, you had 56 cents left. Add that to the $1.18 that was already in your account, and that swells your life savings to a grand total of $1.74!

It's hard to save. It's difficult to put away for the future when we're living in the *now.*

There is one bank account, however, where you can quickly accumulate wealth. It's the First Bank of Good Deeds and Faithful Service to the Lord. This bank doesn't close at 3:00 P.M. You can make deposits twenty-four hours a day, seven days a week, and each deposit is posted immediately. This bank pays the highest interest around, too. Each depositor gets a mansion to live in, mortgage-free, for all eternity. That sure beats three, four, or even ten percent.

Don't get me wrong. It's a good idea to be wise with our money here on earth, to save as much as we can. But the deposits that really count are the ones we make with God.

Thoughts to Ponder:

Why do you think the treasures we lay up in heaven are more important than the ones here on earth?

Do you think God is keeping track of every "deposit" you make in His kingdom? How do you know this?

Bumper Sticker for the Day:

God gives His depositors a lot more than a toaster.

Scripture to Stand On:

"But store up for yourselves treasures in heaven, where moth and rust do not destroy, and where thieves do not break in and steal. For where your treasure is, there your heart will be also."

MATTHEW 6:20-21

Hello Again, Lord ...

Lord, help me to make more deposits in my heavenly account than withdrawals.

Sixty-six
▲▼▲

Follow
the Leader

Has a friend ever let you down? A family member disappointed you? A Christian you respected not lived up to your expectations?

People don't always do what we want—like be perfect. When they fail, we feel as though we've failed, too, because we overestimated their friendship or Christian commitment.

Obviously, we've forgotten one simple fact of life—people aren't faultless. They're going to make mistakes. No matter how infallible we think they are, some day in some way chances are they're going to disappoint us. That's why we have to be very careful about whose life we pattern our actions after.

If you're caravaning to the beach, and the driver in the car in front of you changes his mind, turns around and heads back home, would you follow and then later complain about it? Or would you keep your eyes on the lead car, and ultimately get to the beach and have a good time? You'd follow the leader, of course.

The Bible tells us that we should follow our leader, too—Jesus. "But my eyes are fixed on you, O Sovereign Lord" (Ps 141:8a). He's the only One who won't ever let us down or fail to meet our full expectations. Keep your eyes focused on Him and you won't be disappointed.

Thoughts to Ponder:

Tell about a time when someone let you down or failed to live up to your expectations.

Why is it comforting to know that you can always depend on God?

Bumper Sticker for the Day:

Walking with the Lord requires a lot of eye contact.

Scripture to Stand On:

"My eyes are ever on the Lord."   PSALM 25:15A

Hello Again, Lord...

Lord, You never take Your eyes off me. Help me to keep mine on You.

Sixty-seven
▲▼▲

Divine Backup

You've probably heard the story of Shadrach, Meshach and Abed-nego—three young men of God who were thrown into a fiery furnace for refusing to bow down to an idol (see Daniel 3). God was with them in the midst of the flames and not one hair on their heads was burned. Their clothes didn't even smell of smoke.

God was with Shadrach, Meshach and Abednego in the midst of the fire, but I can't help but wonder why He didn't just put out the flames instead. He could have sent rain from heaven to douse them, or wind to blow them out. He even could have opened the furnace door with His mighty hand and helped those three godly men escape their predicament altogether. After all, one miracle would have been just as easy for Him as the other.

But He chose instead to go with them *through* the fire. They had to go into the fiery furnace, stay in the fiery furnace, and come out of the fiery furnace. No harm came to them, but they had to endure it.

When we go through our own problems and trials, we may wonder why God doesn't just put out the fire or open the furnace door so we can escape. Why should we have to face the flames? For whatever reason—whether it's for our growth in Him or to increase our faith for future tests—He sometimes allows us to stay in the furnace for a while. He doesn't leave us there alone, though. He stays right by us in the midst of the flames, encouraging us. And He sees to it that not one hair of ours is singed, either!

Thoughts to Ponder:

Have you ever gone through something that you wished you could have escaped, but had to go through anyway? What was it?

✎

What did you learn from your experience about trusting God through your trials?

✎

Bumper Sticker for the Day:

Even in the heat of our problems,
God will be there to help us keep our cool.

Scripture to Stand On:

"Yet he saved them for his name's sake, to make his mighty power known."   PSALM 106:8

Hello Again, Lord ...

Lord, help me to remember that You'll always be with me... to help me out of my problems or to see me through them.

Sixty-eight
▲▼▲

Disobedience Ingredients

You give people a rule and chances are they are going to break it. Look at Adam and Eve. They only had two rules to follow—"Don't eat of the Tree of Life" and "Don't eat of the Tree of Knowledge of Good and Evil." There were no other rules. They could stay up as late as they wanted, go wherever they desired in the garden, let as many animals follow them home as they liked. They had no homework, no curfew, no restrictions of any kind, except for those two rules.

So what did they do? They disobeyed one of them. They ate of the Tree of Knowledge of Good and Evil.

Disobedience usually comes with a punishment, and once God confronted them over their disobedience, they had to leave the garden and start fending for themselves.

Was the brief moment it took for them to eat the fruit worth what they paid? I don't think so. Did they learn their lesson? Absolutely. It was too late to get back what they once had, but not too late to ask for forgiveness.

Rationalizing God's laws is the first step toward disobeying them. The serpent manipulated Eve into doing just that. "You will not surely die if you eat of it," the serpent said, tempting her. "God just doesn't want you to be like Him" (see Genesis 3:4).

But God's laws are His laws and they are meant to be obeyed. Not rationalized, analyzed, or even neutralized. Obeyed.

We have every right to live in disobedience. But we might be giving up paradise to do it.

Thoughts to Ponder:

Why do you think obedience is important to God?

Has disobedience ever cost you more than you thought it would?

Is there something you considered doing, even though you knew it was wrong? Had you gone through with it, what do you think disobedience might have cost you?

Bumper Sticker for the Day:

Everything has a price tag... especially disobedience.

Scripture to Stand On:

"If you want to enter life, obey the commandments."

MATTHEW 19:17B

Hello Again, Lord...

Lord, help me to realize that the best way is to obey.

Sixty-nine
▲▼▲

Down to the Wire

Have you noticed how God sometimes rescues us at the very last minute? Just when the problem seems insurmountable, just when we have nowhere else to turn, He comes through.

I'm sure He has a reason for doing this. I think it's so we'll know beyond a shadow of a doubt who won our battle. It's His way of building our faith in Him and helping us learn to trust in His perfect care.

Think about it: God didn't part the Red Sea until Moses was at its bank (see Exodus 14). It would have been easier on Moses' faith had the Lord parted the waters, say, five or ten miles back. The Israelites would have seen the sea separating, thanked Moses for being such a great man of God, then walked jubilantly across.

But God didn't part the Red Sea until the very moment they *needed* to cross. Not a minute before. And I'm sure the closer those Israelites got to that vast body of water, the harder it was on Moses. I can almost hear the grumbling now.

"Okay, great leader, *now* what do we do? You brought us all the way out here in the desert, Pharoah's army is on our tail, and there isn't a single bridge in sight. Who put *you* in charge anyway?"

That's just the remarks to his face. There were probably plenty of snide comments going on behind his back, too.

"What in the world is Moses doing? Does he think that's a mirage ahead of us?"

"Maybe he got some sand in his eyes and he doesn't even see all that water in front of us."

"He's leading us right into the sea. If he thought we all needed a bath, why didn't he just say so?"

Moses had to stand firm in his belief that, since God had brought them this far, He wasn't going to fail them now. After all, the One who created the Red Sea could surely do whatever it took to get His people across it.

And He did.

Thoughts to Ponder:

Think of a situation when God came through for you at the very last minute.

✎

How might that experience give you more faith to trust Him when future problems come your way?

✎

Bumper Sticker for the Day:

When all else fails, He won't.

Scripture to Stand On:

"He will not let your foot slip—he who watches over you will not slumber."   PSALMS 121:3

Hello Again, Lord ...

Lord, help me to remember that even in the last inning, with two outs and two strikes against me, You always come through.

Seventy
▲▼▲

Take My Offering...
Please

When the offering plate comes by, do you reach into your pocket and start singing "Deeper, Deeper" or do you just sit there and sing "Hide Thou Me?"

Have you ever squeezed a dollar bill so tightly before putting it in the offering that you took the curl out of George Washington's hair?

Have you ever written an I.O.U. to God on a tithe envelope?

Even though the Bible tells us that we are to be generous with our giving, it's not easy. Sometimes we carry on an intense mental discussion with ourselves while the offering plate is coming by:

"I really should give my tithe."

"I know, but then that'll only leave me with 90 percent of my babysitting money. God knows I don't get paid enough to watch those kids. They tied me up in a chair, set off stink bombs in my purse, and sprayed Silly String in my hair. And that was just during my job interview!"

"Even so, the Bible says that whatever blessings we have are from God. He only asks us to give a portion back to Him."

If we time this mental discussion just right, we can still be debating the issue with ourselves when the offering plate arrives in front of us. We'll give next week, we rationalize, then pass the plate on down the row. But next week isn't when we should show our appreciation to God for last week's blessings. Why not show our gratefulness today?

Thoughts to Ponder:

What do you think God wants to teach us through the principle of giving?

When we give back to God a portion of His financial blessings, what do you think that says about our thankfulness?

Bumper Sticker for the Day:

The Lord loveth a cheerful giver...
not a tearful one.

Scripture to Stand On:

"Remember this: Whoever sows sparingly will also reap sparingly, and whoever sows generously will also reap generously."

2 CORINTHIANS 9:6

Hello Again, Lord...

Lord, help me to be as generous with what I give to You as You are with what You give to me.

Seventy-one
▲▼▲

One Size Fits All

As a teen, I learned the difference between God's forgiveness and man's forgiveness. It happened at a slumber party. We were playing a game where you go around the room and everyone confesses a wrongdoing. At first, it was pretty innocent. This one had jaywalked. That one had an overdue library book. This one put seaweed in her camp counselor's sleeping bag. Everyone confessed minor infractions, and we all had some good laughs. That is, until one girl got caught up in the game and confessed a "biggie." In our book, it was a clear eleven on a scale of one to ten.

The game wasn't much fun after that. We all said we were tired and went to bed. I don't think I saw anyone talk to that girl again.

Aren't you glad God's forgiveness isn't like that? He not only forgives our minor sins—the socially acceptable ones, the ones that don't raise too many eyebrows. He also forgives the biggies, as well. We can confess those elevens to Him, and not worry that He's going to hold them against us. His blood covers *all* of our sins. When we confess them to Him and ask His forgiveness, it's the sin that gets erased—not His love for us.

Thoughts to Ponder:

Why do you think God's forgiveness is so much better than ours?

Do you think God sees any difference in the size of our sins? Why or why not?

Bumper Sticker for the Day:

God's forgiveness is like a tropical rain storm.
It covers everything.

Scripture to Stand On:

"Though your sins are like scarlet, they shall be as white as snow; though they are red as crimson, they shall be like wool."

ISAIAH 1:18B

Hello Again, Lord...

Lord, though my sins may be varied, Your forgiveness covers them all.

Seventy-two
▲▼▲

Whodunit?

Do you ever feel frustrated because you are doing your best to be good, be kind to others, or change a bad behavior, yet no one notices? You've been cleaning under your bed without being told (and before the ants started picketing). You've been bridling your tongue every time your big brother picks on you. You've been doing your homework at home as you should, instead of doing it while walking down the hall on the way to class. You've been improving your ways, but no one seems to see it. It's disappointing to work diligently at something day in and day out and not have someone comment on our progress. It's discouraging—and sometimes we want to give up.

But we don't have to worry about impressing others with our good deeds or how many bad habits we conquer, or how much work we do for the Lord. We have to impress only one person, and that's the One keeping the books.

The Bible tells us in Ecclesiastes 12:14 that God will bring *every* deed into judgment, even the hidden ones, good or evil. He's got them all written down. God recorded all those times you helped in children's church when it seemed as though the kids were reenacting the battle of Jericho and seeing how many walls they could tumble over. When you shared that last brownie with your little sister even though you wanted to eat the whole thing (and lick the plate, too), God duly noted your sacrifice. Each time you've chosen to do the right thing instead of the wrong, He's made it a matter of record.

So continue doing those good deeds, whether anyone sees them or not. It's all being recorded in Heaven. God's a great bookkeeper. He hasn't missed an entry yet.

Thoughts to Ponder:

Is it better to focus on what God thinks about you or what others think about you? Why?

What comfort do you find in knowing God is happy with you?

Bumper Sticker for the Day:

Good deeds or bad deeds,
God always knows whodunit.

Scripture to Stand On:

"I the Lord search the heart and examine the mind, to reward a man according to his conduct, according to what his deeds deserve."

JEREMIAH 17:10

Hello Again, Lord...

Lord, You're the one I have to please, and the best way I can do that is down on my knees.

Seventy-three
▲▼▲

Walk This Way

Sometimes God leads us down a path that makes us think we need a better travel agent. We take an unexpected turn here, climb a hill there. We can't understand why He didn't choose the easier path that we mapped out for ourselves. Why didn't we get that first job we applied for, instead of having to turn in forty-seven employment applications all over town? Why didn't we pass those cheerleader tryouts on the first try, instead of on the ninth? Why didn't we get a driver's license when we wanted it, instead of failing the test three times (and backing into the Department of Motor Vehicles building once)?

I'm sure the Israelites were baffled when God told Joshua to lead them around the walls of Jericho seven times (see Joshua 6). But they did it anyway. They didn't grumble, "Hey, man, this is so corny. This is the corniest thing we've ever done." They didn't complain, "Come on, Joshua, our feet hurt. Can't we just attack the city and be done with it?" They didn't even worry about how the Jericho Evening News was going to portray them, which, by the way, might have gone something like this: "This just in! Well, folks, it seems the Israelite army is at it again. This time they've been sighted marching around the walls of our city. And they're singing, too. I'm afraid all that wandering around in the desert has gotten to them. According to reports, this is their sixth trip around. There's no cause for alarm, though. City officials have assured us that even if they do try to attack, they'll only be knocking their heads against a block wall."

But they should have worried, because after the Israelites' last trip around the city, the walls of Jericho fell flatter than one of my soufflés. The Israelites conquered the mighty city of Jericho—not because of their strength, but because of their obedience. They trusted that God, their Commander in Chief, was going to win the battle for them. All they had to do was follow orders.

When you think about it, it really is a little foolish not to trust God's leading. After all, we're looking at our journey one step at a time. He's the one with the whole map.

Thoughts to Ponder:

Have you ever been in an airplane as it made its way through heavy clouds? How did you feel about not being able to see very far ahead or bumping through the turbulence?

Were you able to trust the pilot to fly the plane safely? If so, why?

Why do you think it's best to let God lead us rather than choose to go our own way?

Bumper Sticker for the Day:

I may not always know where I'm going,
but the One I'm following does.

Scripture to Stand On:

"The Lord will guide you always." ISAIAH 58:11A

Hello Again, Lord ...

Lord, help me to trust my footsteps to the Maker of the Pathway.

Seventy-four

▲▼▲

Sign of the Time

"**K**eep Out!"

The sign was old and hanging cockeyed on one nail. Surely it no longer applied. Cutting across this field would save me half an hour on my walk home. The split rail fence was badly in need of repair. If they *really* wanted to keep people out, I told myself, they would have maintained it better.

But since I have more chicken in me than Colonel Sanders, I walked cautiously across the field, ready to run at the first sign of the owner.

I didn't have to wait long. After walking only a few minutes, I saw him. He was big, mean-looking, and headed right toward me. Not the owner. His two-thousand-pound bull!

My legs froze and my heart started to pound. That bull was ready to defend his territory; I was ready to faint.

I quickly pulled myself together and nearly broke the sound barrier racing back to that split rail fence. It may have been in need of repair, but I knew if I didn't get on the other side of it, my body would soon be in need of the same thing.

With the bull less than one hundred yards away, I sailed over the fence with a leap that would have qualified me for the Olympics.

Seeing I was no longer fair game, the bull reluctantly retreated. I paused just long enough to catch my breath and take another look at that "Keep Out" sign. It was rusted and old and weatherworn, but it still bore some good advice.

I learned a lesson that day. A good rule is a good rule no matter when it was written.

God's rules are good rules. They may have been written thousands of years ago, but they haven't needed a rewrite yet.

Thoughts to Ponder:

Are there any rules that you thought were irrelevant, but found out later they made pretty good sense?

Why do you think God has given His people certain rules to live by?

What happens when we try to take a shortcut and bypass one of God's rules?

Bumper Sticker for the Day:

If God had thought the Ten Commandments were going to
need updating, He would have written them on
erasable paper, not in stone.

Scripture to Stand On:

"Keep my commandments, and live; and my law as the apple
of thine eye."   PROVERBS 7:2 (KJV)

Hello Again, Lord...

Lord, help me to realize there's no shortcut when it comes to
obeying Your laws.

Seventy-five
▲▼▲

Quiet, Please

"Quiet!"

You've probably heard that word a lot. I know I did as a teenager. But then again, teenagers can get pretty noisy at times. I remember one slumber party I had that got so noisy that our dog sat up and begged for earplugs. And once I was with a youth group that was so loud, the manager of Taco Bell had to ask us to go home. That may not sound so bad, but at the time we were eating at McDonalds four miles away!

Don't get me wrong. I think it's great to have a good time. I love to laugh and have fun myself. But quietness can be a good thing, too. If we're always in the middle of a party, if there's always noise and conversation going on around us, it's hard to hear that still, small voice of God.

So why not turn that radio down and lower the volume on the television set. Ask your parents to hold all your phone calls and tell your visitors that you'll have to catch them later. Right now you want to spend a little quiet time with Someone who's been patiently waiting to spend some quiet time with you.

Thoughts to Ponder:

Why do you think it's important for us to set aside some quiet time to spend with the Lord?

When is the best time of day for you to spend quiet moments with God?

Bumper Sticker for the Day:

Sometimes our heavenly Father would like
His children to sit still, too.

Scripture to Stand On:

"There is a time for everything, and a season for every activity under heaven... a time to be silent and a time to speak."

ECCLESIASTES 3:1,7

Hello Again, Lord...

Lord, remind me that it's in those quiet times with You that I can hear so much.

Seventy-six
▲▼▲

It's About Time

Did you know that timing is important? If a brownie recipe reads "bake brownies for thirty-five minutes," it means thirty-five minutes. Not ten minutes (unless you want to eat them with a soup spoon). Not four-and-a-half hours (unless you want to eat them with the fire department).

Timing is important in football, too. If the quarterback tosses the ball too soon (like while his teammate is tying his shoe), the other team could intercept the ball and score a touchdown.

Timing is important in diving as well. If you do that triple somersault with a half twist while the pool is being drained, you're going to end up making quite an impression. Not on the spectators. In the cement.

Did you know God has His own timing? He knows exactly when to answer our prayers. Perhaps we want something right now. It may seem like He's not listening. We may even think He's saying "no." Instead, what He might be saying is "slow"— slow down and rest in His timing. He *wants* to answer our prayers, if they're in accordance with His will. But He'll answer them when it's the right time. The perfect time. *His* time.

Thoughts to Ponder:

Have you ever prayed a prayer which wasn't answered in your time, but rather in God's time? Explain.

Why do you think it's important that we trust God's timing in our lives?

Bumper Sticker for the Day:

Set your clock by God's time.
It's always 100 percent accurate.

Scripture to Stand On:

"But I trust in you, O Lord; I say, 'You are my God.' My times are in your hands."   PSALM 31:14-15A

Hello Again, Lord...

Lord, You're never too late or too early. You always come through on time.

Seventy-seven
▲▼▲

Read Any Good Books Lately?

In high school I once tried writing a book report on a book I hadn't read. I don't recommend it. I guessed at the setting, incorrectly listed the protagonist as the antagonist, made up the plot, and basically proved I knew little about the book. The only information I had correct was the title and number of pages.

Sometimes we do that with the Bible, too. We're satisfied to know just a little bit about it. We know its title—Holy Bible. We can easily find Psalms and Matthew, but let a preacher use Obadiah or Nahum as his text, and we'll be flipping through the pages until the closing hymn.

We might even find ourselves talking about Jonah and the Ark, or how Moses marched around the walls of Jericho seven times. We could refer to the Six Commandments, Daniel and the whale, or Adam in the lion's den.

By not really reading the Book, we run the risk of getting the plot wrong, the quotes wrong, the truth wrong.

The Bible is too good of a book to merely skim through. It's full of action and adventure. If you don't believe me, just check out the stories of Gideon, Joshua, and Moses. For sci-fi fans, it has some of the best sci-*non*fi around. Just turn to Revelation and read about the future.

The Bible has suspense, history, humor, and plenty of good advice. As a matter of fact, it's the best "how-to" book on the market. It covers how to succeed in life, how to get along with others, how to find happiness. It's all in there.

Don't take any shortcuts when it comes to this book. It deserves to be read cover to cover, page by page, word for word. It's a great way to get to know the Author, too.

Thoughts to Ponder:

Do you think it's important to spend time reading God's Word? Why?

✎

Are you spending as much time in the Word as you should? If not, what steps can you take to change that?

✎

Bumper Sticker for the Day:

If they dusted your Bible for fingerprints,
would they find any fresh ones?

Scripture to Stand On:

"Your word is a lamp to my feet and a light for my path."

PSALM 119:105

Hello Again, Lord...

Lord, help me to honor You daily by spending time in Your Word.

Seventy-eight

▲▼▲

Growing Pains

When I was a child, I was so bowlegged I could stand with my feet together and still hold a beach ball between my knees. To correct the problem, I had to wear braces to bed every night. I'd cry and beg my parents to remove them, but they made me wear them anyway. They knew it was best for me in the long run.

Today, I don't remember any of those tears or tantrums. But I *am* walking on a straight pair of legs, thanks to Mom and Dad's persistency.

In junior high, I began having lots of growing pains. My mother's remedy for these was a healthy dose of cod-liver oil. Now, if you don't know what cod-liver oil tastes like, let me just say it'll never be a Baskin Robbins "Flavor of the Month." It was awful! It could make you gag faster than one of my casseroles. I used to hide in my bedroom for hours to avoid taking it. But Mom would always find me and make me take my medicine.

As horrible as it was, I have to admit it did help. The pains seemed to lessen, and all that running from Mom had to have definite cardiovascular benefits.

Growing up isn't always painless. Growing up in the Lord isn't either. Sometimes we may have to take some pretty foul tasting medicine, or put our own desires in a spiritual brace for a while to make sure we grow up properly. Sure, we might whimper and cry with the discomfort. We might even attempt to hide. But the best thing to do is trust our heavenly Father and believe that, He, too, knows what's best for us. In the long run, we'll thank Him for it.

Thoughts to Ponder:

Have you gone through something that was painful at the time, but from which you now see you've grown? Explain.

Why do you think that growing up sometimes involves pain?

Bumper Sticker for the Day:

If you're not having a few growing pains,
you may not be growing.

Scripture to Stand On:

"And the God of all grace, who called you to his eternal glory in Christ, after you have suffered a little while, will himself restore you and make you strong, firm and steadfast."

1 PETER 5:10

Hello Again, Lord ...

Lord, keep me from throwing tantrums to get my own way, for Your way will always be better for me.

Seventy-nine
▲▼▲

Happy, Happy Birthday

I have two birthdays. Actually, it works out pretty nicely. If anyone forgets to buy me a gift on one birthday, they get a second chance.

I should explain. For the first half of my life, my birthday was September 2. It's on all my school records, my baptismal certificate, it's written in the family Bible—it was September 2.

When I needed a copy of my birth certificate for my marriage license, however, I was surprised to read that my real birthday was September *1*, a day earlier! Imagine doing that to any woman—making her older than she thinks she is, even if it is by just a day!

My mother and father were just as surprised as I was. They thought for sure I had been born on the second.

"Maybe I was so good and quiet, you didn't notice me until the following day," I suggested.

"No, that couldn't be it," my parents insisted. "Maybe you were born at midnight, and they just listed it on the first."

Checking the birth certificate again proved that theory wrong. I didn't hold it against my mom, though. I was the last of five children. It's a miracle she remembered her *own* birthday.

I have a third birthday, too. It's the day that I invited the Lord into my life. I was only six years old, but it was one of the most important decisions I've ever made.

Three birthdays... ummm... now no one has an excuse for not remembering at least *one* of them.

Thoughts to Ponder:

Do you remember when you made your decision to follow Christ? Describe that moment.

How has that decision affected your life?

Bumper Sticker for the Day:

Birthdays are important, but not as important as
who you're living each year for.

Scripture to Stand On:

"And this is the testimony: God has given us eternal life, and this life is in his Son."

1 JOHN 5:11

Hello Again, Lord...

Lord, thank You for being in my life. May You always feel welcome and appreciated.

Eighty
▲▼▲

The Caretaker

"**W**ill you watch my things while I go stand in line?" you say to a trusted friend who doesn't want to ride the triple loop, double corkscrew roller coaster with two eighty-foot drops.

Your friend agrees, and you hurry to stand in a line that wraps around the amusement park *twice*.

After fifteen minutes, though, you start to worry. Sure, your friend is responsible. You've trusted her with your belongings before and nothing has ever happened to them. But what if ...

So you get out of line and return to your friend.

"Are you still watching my stuff?" you ask, even though it's perfectly obvious that she is.

"I'm not going anywhere," your friend assures you. "Go on, have a good time."

You return to the ride, but by now you've lost your place and have to go to the end of the line. This time you make it halfway through the line before the worrying sets in again.

So you get out of line to check just one more time, and find your friend doing exactly what she promised. But you still can't let go.

"Maybe I should take my things on the ride with me," you say, filling your arms item by item. "Don't get me wrong. I trust you. It's just that I'd feel better if I keep them with me."

With your things safely in your hands, you get back in line

once again (at the end, of course), and try to relax. But you can't because all the things you've insisted on carrying are getting heavier and heavier by the minute.

Sound crazy? You say you'd never do anything like that? Well, we do it every time we leave our cares in God's hands, then keep going back and trying to carry them ourselves. Sure, we trust Him. But what if...

Not fully trusting God with our cares is like hiring a sumo wrestler to help us move a piano, then telling him to wait in the truck while we do it ourselves. It's keeping the burden on ourselves when his shoulders are so much bigger.

Thoughts to Ponder:

When we give God our cares, do we need to keep checking on them? Why not?

Why do you think God wants us to give Him our burdens?

Bumper Sticker for the Day:
When God said to cast all our cares on Him,
He didn't mean for them to be on a fishing line
so we can reel them back in.

Scripture to Stand On:
"Cast all your anxiety on him because he cares for you."

1 PETER 5:7

Hello Again, Lord...
Lord, let me remember when I send my cares to You, it should be a one-way trip.

Eighty-one

▲▼▲

Simply Put

I finally went shopping for a computer, something I had been putting off for years. When I walked into the computer store I remembered why I'd been putting it off. When it comes to computers, I'm illiterate. I don't know my disk drive from a scenic drive, and to me, RAM isn't a computer term—it's what I do to the car in front of me when my brakes give out. I know a megabite is what my teenage son takes when he's trying to down a Big Mac, a floppy disk is what I'll have if I leave my hard disk out in the sun too long and it melts, and "booting the system" is how novice computer users like me get the computer up and running (make sure you're wearing hard boots, though, to avoid toe injury).

As you can see, I'm not ready for a computer. Besides, I don't really want another mouse in the house.

Thank goodness the gospel is simple and easy to follow. I don't need fourteen instruction books or a six-month training course just to comprehend its message. "For God so loved the world, that he gave his only begotten Son, that whosoever believeth in him should not perish, but have everlasting life" (Jn 3:16, KJV). There's nothing complicated or confusing about that. It's clear-cut and easy to understand.

The gospel—it really is user friendly.

Thoughts to Ponder:

Why do you suppose God made His plan of salvation so easy to understand?

✎

In what ways do we try to complicate it?

✎

Bumper Sticker for the Day:

God's Word doesn't go over your head.
It penetrates your heart.

Scripture to Stand On:

"Then he opened their minds so they could understand the Scriptures."

LUKE 24:45

Hello Again, Lord...

Lord, thank You for the simplicity of Your message.

Eighty-two

▲ ▼ ▲

Help Wanted

Did you know that it's fun to do the Lord's work? No, that isn't a misprint. It really is *fun*. It's a blessing, it's enriching, it's rewarding, it's all those things. But it's fun, too.

When my husband and I were children's church directors, we planned a program where several parents from the congregation shared about their jobs with the children. On one Sunday, we had a policeman. On another, a carpenter. Another week, we had a mechanic.

One of my favorites was the father who owned his own crane company. You should have seen the children's eyes when they heard that crane pull into the church driveway. The father sent word to us, though, that he would need about fifteen minutes to get things ready. So, we led the children in a few choruses, served some refreshments, then walked on out to the parking lot to see the crane.

What we saw brought forth screams of delight from the children. It brought forth screams from the directors, too, but they weren't of delight. They were of shock!

There, dangling one hundred feet in the air, was our *car!* It was belted onto the crane, and swinging back and forth in the wind.

Once the shock wore off (and our car was safely back on the ground), we all had a good laugh over it.

It is a lot of good fun doing God's work. Sure, there are times when it's serious, but it can be fun, too.

Try volunteering your time. The church needs all sorts of workers. Not just adult workers, either. I wrote and directed my first comedy program for a church congregation when I was nineteen years old. I've been active in church work ever since. I love it. You will, too. It's a great job. God's a terrific boss. And just wait until you hear about His retirement plan!

Thoughts to Ponder:

Are you already helping in the Lord's work? If so, in what capacity?

If not, is there an area where you might like to help? What is it?

Do you think God can use each one of us, no matter what our talents? Why do you feel as you do?

Bumper Sticker for the Day:
In God's work, the layoff rate is zero.

Scripture to Stand On:
"The harvest is plentiful but the workers are few."   MATTHEW 9:37

Hello Again, Lord ...

Lord, help me to dedicate whatever talents I might have to Your service.

Eighty-three
▲ ▼ ▲

Trust Me

It's important to be careful where you place your trust.

Some barbers say "trust me" as half of your eyebrow falls into your lap.

Some dentists say "trust me" as they drill down deeper than Exxon.

Some postal workers say "trust me," stamp your package "Fragile," and then drop-kick it into the parcel bin.

Some manicurists say "trust me" as they push your cuticles back to your elbow.

Some mechanics say "trust me," then make your engine purr like a kitten...with strep throat.

Some friends say "trust me" as they borrow your favorite shirt, accidentally wash it in *hot* water, then hand you back a swatch.

A lot of people say "trust me," but don't quite earn your trust. They fall short of their promises, and leave you wishing you hadn't placed your faith in them in the first place.

Aren't you glad, though, that when God says "trust Me," you can?

Thoughts to Ponder:

Tell about a time you placed your trust in someone who proved not to be very trustworthy.

Why do you think where we place our trust is important?

Bumper Sticker for the Day:

"In God We Trust"—if our dollar can say it, so can we.

Scripture to Stand On:

"He *is* a shield unto them that put their trust in Him."

PROVERBS 30:5B (KJV)

Hello Again, Lord ...

Lord, help me to remember that trust which is placed in You is never misplaced trust.

Eighty-four

▲▼▲

Teamwork

The Lord has one team. It's not divided into the Baptists versus the Presbyterians, or the Lutherans against the Methodists. It's *one* team, united.

Who's on the team and who's not on the team? That's as plain to see as the blemishes in my senior picture. Jesus said, "He who is not with me is against me" (Mt 12:30a).

Common sense tells us that a team that is united is going to be more effective than one that isn't. If the first baseman doesn't want to work with the shortstop, he doesn't have to. But it's going to be hard for him to catch all those balls that fly between second and third base. If the pitcher chooses to ignore the catcher, that's his decision. But he's going to get awfully tired running back and forth to catch his own pitches.

"But just look at that catcher. He uses different equipment than the rest of us. He can't be on our team."

"And you can't tell me that shortstop is on our team. He never runs after the ball like us outfielders."

"Have you seen that third baseman hit? All he ever does is bunt. Sure, it gets him on base and he eventually scores, but that's not how *we* do it. He can't possibly be on our team either."

Anyone who knows baseball knows you need the *whole* team to play. The pitcher, the shortstop, the outfielders—you need everyone working together to be effective.

God cares more about our hearts than our doctrinal differences. What He really wants to know is—are you for Him or against Him? Are you on His team or not?

Thoughts to Ponder:

Why do you think more can be accomplished when a team works together?

What are the disadvantages of a baseball team made up of only shortstops? Or only outfielders? Or only pitchers?

Bumper Sticker of the Day:

Division belongs in math class, not in God's family.

Scripture to Stand On:

"Make every effort to keep the unity of the Spirit through the bond of peace."   EPHESIANS 4:3

Hello Again, Lord...

Lord, help me to use this final inning to add to Your kingdom, rather than divide it.

Eighty-five
▲ ▼ ▲

Forever Hold
Your Peace

Remember the story of Peter walking on the water to meet Jesus? He did fine until he took his eyes off the Lord. Once he did that, he had the buoyancy of an anchor. He went down and down and down...until he called out to Jesus, who rescued him.

But Peter didn't start to sink until he changed his focus. As long as he had his eyes on Jesus, he could've faith-surfed the entire Sea of Galilee. But after only a few steps out of the boat, he started seeing the wind, instead of the One who controlled it.

God wants us to trust Him in the midst of our waves, too. Whether we're riding the four-foot swells or the ten-foot swells, we're to put our hand in His. We shouldn't focus on the depth of the water, the size of the sharks, or the harshness of the winds. We shouldn't lose our faith after just a few steps out of the boat either. We're to keep the faith and keep our eyes on Him, ready to ride whatever ups and downs come our way. If we stay focused on the Prince of Peace, we can't help but stay afloat.

Thoughts to Ponder:

Can you think of a problem you had to face in which it was hard to keep your eyes on the Lord? What was it?

✎

Why do you think it's important to keep our eyes on the Lord in the midst of our problems?

✎

Bumper Sticker for the Day:

It's easy to walk in faith inside the boat.
It's those steps outside that get a little more difficult.

Scripture to Stand On:

"May the God of hope fill you with all joy and peace as you trust in him."   ROMANS 15:13

Hello Again, Lord...

Lord, help me to keep my eyes on You and off the waves.

Eighty-Six

▲▼▲

Happy Endings

A lot of situations are intended to be the closing scene, the finale, "The End." Here are a few:

When gossip reaches our ears, that should be "The End." It should stop right then and there. It shouldn't continue another minute.

When someone asks for our forgiveness, that should be "The End." We shouldn't keep rerunning their offense to this friend and that friend, changing the script a little as we go. When we offer someone our forgiveness, that scene is over. It's "The End."

When we ask forgiveness from the Lord, we should consider it "The End." The end of our guilt, the end of dwelling on what we've done wrong. It's "The End" of that sin as far as He's concerned. It should be "The End" of it as far as we're concerned, too.

When we give the Lord our troubles and cares, that should be "The End" of our worrying. Why stress out over each and every problem when He's carrying them?

If we'll learn to face our day with the script God wants us to use, the one He's written, we'll be able to wrap up those scenes exactly where we're supposed to. After all, with God directing our lives, how can we help but have plenty of happy endings?

Thoughts to Ponder:

Are you letting something continue that should have ended long ago? If so, what is it?

List some of the things God promises will end when we bring them to Him.

Bumper Sticker for the Day:

Sometimes the best way to bounce back
from a problem is to drop it.

Scripture to Stand On:

"The end of a matter is better than its beginning."

ECCLESIASTES 7:8A

Hello Again, Lord...

Lord, help me to know which behaviors need an ending and which ones need a sequel.

Eight-seven
▲▼▲

Questions
and Answers

Have you ever questioned God? Wondered why He allowed something terrible to happen? A close relative dies, a good friend is in a horrible car accident, someone from school is diagnosed with an incurable disease. Why is life so painfully hard to understand at times?

It's difficult, if not impossible, to fully answer questions like these because none of us will completely understand God's planning and timing until we get to heaven and ask Him about it. He'll gladly answer every one of our questions then, and when He does, all the pieces of the puzzle will at last fall neatly into place.

A few of our questions might even be answered by just taking a look around up there. We might meet someone who came to know the Lord because of the testimony our friend showed throughout all his earthly trials. We may run into another whose life was eternally changed after the death of our relative. There's no telling what kind of stories are going to unfold before our eyes.

Until that day comes, though, we just have to be like we were when we were children riding in the family car. We didn't understand every turn Mom or Dad took back then, but we rested in the fact that *they* knew what they were doing and they always got us home.

Thoughts to Ponder:

What questions do you have that you would like to ask God?

✎

Even when we don't understand something that happens in our lives, how can we know that we can still trust God's love for us?

✎

Bumper Sticker for the Day:

God makes it easy to trust Him.
We're the ones who try to make it hard.

Scripture to Stand On:

"The Lord is good, a refuge in times of trouble. He cares for those who trust in him."   NAHUM 1:7

Hello Again, Lord...

Lord, help me not to question Your wisdom, but only walk in Your love.

Eighty-eight
▲▼▲

For Crying Out Loud

Did you know that there are different kinds of tears? There are the ones babies cry when they're hungry, the ones some toddlers (and a few adults) cry when they don't get their way, and the ones that come from smoke inhalation at one of my sit-down dinners.

The most painful tears, though, are the private ones—the ones we think no one else sees. The ones that fall when we're alone in our room, our car, or in some other private place. For whatever reason, we've been keeping this particular pain all to ourselves. We haven't yet shared it with anyone—not our parents, our brother or sister, not even our best friend.

But we're not really crying those tears alone. God is there right beside us. How do we know that? The Bible tells us in Matthew 10:30 that He knows the number of hairs on our heads. If we can't lose a single split end without God knowing about it, do you really think one of our tears can fall unnoticed by Him?

That's what's so terrific about God. We can tell Him *anything*. We can open up to Him when we feel we can't open up to anyone else. We can trust Him with those parts of our life we're afraid to share with others. We can be real with Him because His love for us is real.

Thoughts to Ponder:

Do you have pain in your life that only you and God know about? Have you been able to talk to Him about it? If not, why not?

✎

Why do you suppose God wanted us to know that He's counted the number of hairs on our heads? What point was He making?

✎

Bumper Sticker for the Day:

Anyone can dry a tear. God heals the broken heart.

Scripture to Stand On:

"Your love, O Lord, reaches to the heavens, your faithfulness to the skies."   PSALM 36:5

Hello Again, Lord...

Lord, help me to remember that You want to carry *all* my burdens... even my private ones.

Eighty-nine

▲▼▲

No Slumber Party

I've chaperoned quite a few slumber parties, and if I've learned anything, I've learned that very little slumbering goes on at most of them. In fact, the only reason to bring a sleeping bag to a slumber party is so your friends will have some place to put the rubber snake and ice cubes.

I chaperoned at one Friday night slumber party where everyone stayed awake until the sun came up... Tuesday morning! That was bad enough, but can you imagine not sleeping for a week, a month, even years? Physically, we couldn't do it. We'd be falling asleep in our pepperoni pizza, or catching a few winks in the punch bowl. We could try propping our eyes open with a couple of breadsticks, but sooner or later, they would become weary and close whether we wanted them to or not.

God's eyes never close. He watches over us every minute of every day. He's watching long after the test pattern has appeared on the television set. He's already awake when that car alarm down the street goes off and wakes up everyone else in the neighborhood. He never sleeps, he never slumbers. You won't catch him dozing on the job, or trying to take a quick nap when you need Him most. He's never tired, and He never tires of watching over us.

Thoughts to Ponder:

What's the longest you've ever been able to stay awake?

Is it comforting to you to know that God never sleeps? Why?

Bumper Sticker for the Day:

Aren't you glad God doesn't keep banking hours?

Scripture to Stand On:

"He who watches over you will not slumber."   PSALM 121:3

Hello Again, Lord...

Lord, thank You that I can call on You whenever I want, and never worry about waking You up.

Ninety
▲▼▲

Roll the Credits

When God helps us through a trial, He wants the credit. It's only fair. He deserves it.

Remember Gideon? His story is found in Judges 6 and 7. The Midianites were oppressing the Israelites, and it was Gideon's mission to conquer them. God promised to go with the Israelites into battle, but He wanted to make sure they didn't boast of their own might. He wanted them to admit who it was who gave them the victory.

So God told Gideon that his army was too large and that he needed to let those soldiers who were afraid go home. (They wouldn't be counted AWOL. They could just bail out on this one.)

Gideon did as God said and twenty-two thousand men went home! That left Gideon with less than one-third of his original army. But God still wanted to make sure the Israelites didn't say it was their military expertise, their sophisticated weaponry, or their brilliant battle plan that conquered the Midianites.

God had Gideon make a few more military cutbacks. He told him to take the troops down to the water for a drink. Only those who lapped the water with their hands to their mouths were to go into battle. Did that leave seven thousand men? five thousand? one thousand?

It left Gideon with only three hundred men! And you know what? The Israelites won! Why? For one reason and one reason only—God was on their side.

God doesn't want us to forget who brings us through our battles, either. When they're over, He wants the credit. It's only fair. He deserves it.

Thoughts to Ponder:

Has God brought you through something that you forgot to give Him the credit for? If so, give Him credit now.

✎

Why is it important for us to realize that it's God who wins our battles?

✎

Bumper Sticker for the Day:

When they do the movie of your life,
make sure the credits are correct.

Scripture to Stand On:

"I will praise you, O Lord, with all my heart; I will tell of all your wonders."

PSALM 9:1

Hello Again, Lord...

Lord, help me to always give credit where credit is due, especially when it belongs to You.

Another Book of Interest by Martha Bolton

Honey, The Carpet Needs Weeding Again!
Martha Bolton

Enter into the zany world of award-winning comedy writer Martha Bolton, where today's frustrations are transformed into tomorrow's laughs.

Honey, The Carpet Needs Weeding Again! promotes an outlook that takes life—and ourselves—less seriously. Says Charlene Ann Baumbich, author of *How to Eat Humble Pie and Not Get Indigestion,* "Martha Bolton knows how to grab our tense faces and, through her anecdotal adventures, story-tell them into laughter, Any woman who boldly admits that changing the sheets is a waste of energy is definitely a heroine of mine!" **$7.99**